PICTORIAL HISTORY OF AMERICAN SPORTS

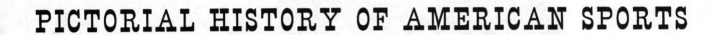

Pictorial History

# of American Sports

From Colonial Times To The Present

THIRD EDITION, REVISED

JOHN DURANT and OTTO BETTMANN

A. S. Barnes and Company

A. S. Barnes and Co., Inc.
Cranbury, New Jersey

Thomas Yoseloff Ltd
108 New Bond Street
London W1Y OQX, England

ISBN 0-498-01461-4

Printed in the United States of America

To Alice who designed every page

Introduction

As things turned out, John Durant's and Dr. Otto Bettmann's story really got under way when a Seneca banged an Ojibway over the head in the first inter-regional lacrosse match several hundred years ago, and one of the many remarkable things you will notice about the story is the number of obstacles it has successfully encountered. Almost at the start, for instance, there was the opposition of Governor Bradford of the Plymouth Colony, with his ban on "gameing or revelling in ye streets," which was no way to encourage curve ball pitching in early-day Massachusetts. Ever since, in one way or another, American sports have flirted at intervals with disaster—the larcenous antics that periodically afflict boxing, the lesser scandals and then the major one that almost finished professional baseball, the curious devices developed by technology to make a horse run faster or slower. To withstand both the self-righteous sour pusses and the more sinister operators any institution needs vitality and ingenuity, and these qualities are—as Mr. Durant and Dr. Bettmann prove so effectively—precisely what American sports have had in abundance.

As they go about their task of demonstrating this in crisp prose and absorbing pictures, the authors arrive at a scheme that happily must appeal alike to the novice, the information-packed expert, and the sentimental antiquarian who vows there never was a fighter who belonged in the same ring with John C. Heenan, the Benicia Boy. Each of them will learn something in this volume. Many a recognized boxing authority, it is to be suspected, will never have seen a photograph of a bare-knuckle fight until he comes upon the one here of the Sullivan-Kilrain fracas. The younger generation, whether reading about the velocipedes ("bone shakers") their dauntless ancestors rode, or gazing upon football players who survived the flying wedge, will behold in these shattering experiences the fortitude that allowed this country to expand from one coast to the other. For the sentimentalists, the names and faces come flocking back in all-star parade: Thorpe and Cobb, Nurmi the Phantom Finn and Grange the Galloping Ghost, the dashing Mlle. Lenglen and the astonishing Boston society girl, Eleanora Sears, the Babe on his great shot-calling day in the 1932 World Series, and the most enduring champion of all, Willie Hoppe, who declined to admit that time could touch a billiard cue. Yet another group will be grateful simply for the odd tidbits with which the authors have decorated corners of their tome. I don't know why, but somehow it is rewarding to know that Jesse James subscribed to *The Police Gazette*, and that in 1834 baserunners ran clockwise around the diamond, even as baserunners were known to do at Ebbets Field, Brooklyn, in the Golden Nineteen Twenties.

So the "revelling in ye streets" led to something vastly worth recording, and here it is in a book that is like a long, good walk through a finely arranged gallery. There has been nothing like this until now. It was worth waiting for.

John K. Hutchens

The Contents

Picture Credits and Acknowledgments

Our thanks are due to the following organizations and individuals who have graciously permitted us the use of picture material in their possession.

Baseball Hall of Fame
Esquire Magazine
Library of Congress
New York Giants
New York Public Library
Racquet and Tennis Club

Rhode Island School of Design
Rutgers University Football Museum
U. S. Golf Association
J. H. Whitney
Whitney Museum of Art
Yale University Library

Listed below are the agencies whose pictures were used in this book. The numerals following their names are page references. Illustrations not credited are from the collections of the authors: The Bettmann Archive and the library of old sporting books owned by John and Alice Durant.

Acme Newspictures:

p. 95 (bt); p. 105; p. 110; p. 112 (top); p. 113 (top); p. 115 (bt); p. 124; p. 144; p. 148 (right); p. 152; p. 153 (top); p. 156; p. 157 (left); p. 160; p. 161; p. 162; p. 163 (right); p. 164; p. 174 (right); p. 175 (bt left); p. 192; p. 193; p. 195 (bt); p. 196; p. 197 (top); p. 217; p. 218 (right); p. 220; p. 221 (bt); p. 222 (right); p. 223; p. 238; p. 241; p. 242 (right); p. 243 (except top); p. 245; p. 272 (top); p. 273.

European Picture Service:

p. 103; p. 104 (top); p. 109 (right); p. 122 (left); p. 136 (left); p. 142; p. 186; p. 187 (bt); p. 194; p. 252; p. 254 (left); p. 274 (top).

Frendy Photos:

p. 119 (top).

International News Service:

p. 99 (bt); p. 112 (bt); p. 113 (bt); p. 115 (top); p. 121 (bt); p. 131 (left); p. 133; p. 145; p. 155 (top); p. 158; p. 159; p. 163 (left); p. 176; p. 179; p. 187 (top); p. 204; p. 205 (except top left); p. 207 (bt); p. 214; p. 215 (left); p. 218 (left); p. 219; p. 222 (left); p. 226; p. 229 (right); p. 231; p. 240; p. 242 (left); p. 243 (top); p. 249; p. 251; p. 253; p. 261 (top); p. 264 (bt); p. 266; p. 272; p. 276.

Keystone View Company:

p. 116 (top); p. 119 (bt); p. 120 (top); p. 121 (top); p. 122 (right); p. 123; p. 130 (right); p. 134 (top); p. 136 (right); p. 146 (bt); p. 147; p. 148 (left); p. 154; p. 155 (bt); p. 173; p. 177; p. 183 (right); p. 188; p. 189; p. 190; p. 197 (bt); p. 203; p. 207 (top); p. 225; p. 227; p. 229

(left); p. 233 (left); p. 237 (bt); p. 247 (top); p. 248 (top); p. 254 (right); p. 256 (bt); p. 257 (top); p. 258; p. 267; p. 278.

Frederick Lewis:

p. 104 (bt); p. 139 (bt); p. 184; p. 200; p. 201; p. 212; p. 213 (top).

Miami News:

p. 283; p. 296.

Underwood and Underwood:

p. 165 (bt); p. 170; p. 171; p. 175 (top); p. 175 (bt).

United Press International:

p. 294; p. 295; p. 297.

Wide World Photos:

p. 94; p. 114 (top); p. 116 (left); p. 120 (bt); p. 125 (bt); p. 137; p. 149; p. 151; p. 153 (bt); p. 157 (right); p. 165 (top); p. 166; p. 167; p. 168 (bt); p. 169; p. 174 (left); p. 178 (top); p. 180; p. 181; p. 183 (left); p. 185; p. 191; p. 195 (top); p. 199 (bt); p. 202; p. 205 (top left); p. 206; p. 208; p. 209; p. 213 (bt); p. 215 (right); p. 216; p. 224; p. 228; p. 230; p. 232; p. 233 (right); p. 234 (top); p. 235; p. 236; p. 237 (top); p. 246; p. 247 (bt); p. 248 (bt); p. 250; p. 255; p. 257 (bt); p. 259; p. 260; p. 261 (bt); p. 262; p. 263; p. 265; p. 268; p. 269; p. 270; p. 271; p. 274 (bt); p. 275; p. 277; p. 279; p. 281; p. 282; p. 284; p. 285; p. 286; p. 287; p. 288; p. 289; p. 290; p. 291; p. 292; p. 293; p. 298; p. 299; p. 300; p. 301; p. 302; p. 303; p. 304; p. 305; p. 306; p. 307; p. 308; p. 309; p. 310; p. 311.

PICTORIAL HISTORY OF AMERICAN SPORTS

CHAPTER ONE
Captain Smith To General Grant
1607–1870

Sports got off to a poor start in the New World. The first settlers who came to these shores in the seventeenth century had never been a part of the sporting life of Merry England. They were, in the main, peasants, servants and craftsmen who brought with them a strong aversion for the pleasures of the English landed nobility. Their resentment, no doubt born of envy, was expressed by a fanatical intolerence of all frivolous pastimes. And sport was a frivolous pastime. Any form of recreation had to be justified as a stern duty. Thus, a man could fish and hunt but only as a means of supplying the larder, not as a sport. Early New England laws forbade bowls, quoits, all tavern sports, card playing and dancing. Macauly hit it right when he quipped that the Puritans banned the sport of bear-baiting, not because of the pain it caused the bear, but because of the pleasure it gave to the spectators.

New England, however, was not long to be devoid of all amusements. Following the Great Migration (1630–1640) when 16,000 people arrived in Massachusettes—only a quarter of whom were church members—a few sports and amusements began to come out in the open. On Training Day, for instance, which was a periodic mustering of all able bodied men of the town, there was target practice, wrestling, running and jumping contests. But these affairs, you may be sure, were staged only after the boys got through drilling. As the Colony swelled its ranks with non-Puritans the Blue Laws became less forceable. Still, the New England sports picture was grim compared to other sections of the New World.

A traveller journeying through the Colonies in the eighteenth Century could not fail to notice the increasing activity of sports from the moment he got out of New England and progressed southwards. In the more urbane middle Colonies containing the key cities of New York and Philadelphia, he would find horse racing, bowls, ice skating carnivals, cock fighting, golf, boat racing, cricket and other sports frowned upon in New England. And in the southern Colonies he might even be shocked, as were many visitors from the North and Europe, by the manner in which sports dominated the lives of the people. They seemed to have time for little else in the upper South, particularly in Virginia. Wealthy planters, imitating the life of the English gentry, had their blooded horses and imported stock for racing and fox hunting. They raised prize gamecocks for the pit and trained slaves to champion them in the ring. There was heavy betting among the planters on these contests, the loser often paying off with a batch of slaves. A glimpse of southern sporting life toward the close of the Eighteenth Century caused the visiting Marquis of Chastellux to frown, "Horse racing, cock fighting and boxing matches are standing amusements, for which they neglected all business."

The Marquis would have been further pained if he had returned a generation later and witnessed the remarkable change that was taking place in American sports. Call it the rise of spectator sports. As early as the 1820's crowds ranging from 20,000 to 100,000 were turning out to watch professional foot races, regattas and horse races. The growth of the cities was responsible for this, the shifting of population from country to town.

From Captain John Smith of Jamestown to General Grant represents more than 250 years, the longest period in time of any of the five chapters in this book. But it is the shortest chapter in number of pages. For in the first two and a half centuries of our history sports developed at a snail's pace and it was not until General Grant's time that they began to come into their own.

The original and most universal game of the American Indians was a stick and ball game which the French explorers called lacrosse. The Indians knew it as baggataway, and it was played from Canada to Florida and west to the great plains. A furious, bone-breaking affair, the idea of the game was to get the ball into the other side's goal by running with it or throwing it—as it is played today. The Indians, however, often had several hundred men on a side.

George Catlin, the American artist and author who lived among the Indians in the 1830's, drew this picture of a brave playing the Choctaw (southeastern United States) version of the game. Note the two webbed bats, or crosses. Northern Indians used only one crosse. The ball was deerskin, stuffed hard with hair, and the players were skillful enough to keep it in the air for long periods at a time. It was, and still is, a rugged game, demanding skill, speed, and endurance.

3

The bishop's crosier (left), a pastoral staff symbolic of his office as shepherd, may have given the name "lacrosse" to the ancient Indian game. According to some authorities, the curved stick used by the Indians reminded the French pioneers of a bishop's crosier and they called the implement *la crosse*.

Lacrosse was only one of the many games played by the American aborigines, as the picture below shows. It was drawn by John White, an English artist who visited Virginia in 1585 and was the first man to make an eye-witness, on-the-spot-drawing of North American Indians. Here, to quote the artist, "They are trained to run races and a prize is given to the one who shows the greatest endurance in the contest. They also practice a great deal with bow and arrow. They play a game in which they cast a ball at a square target placed on the top of a high tree, and they take great pleasure in hunting and fishing."

This picture is supposed to portray the sporting life of the Jamestown Colony in the days of Captain John Smith. It wasn't like this, however. The artist must have drawn this from his imagination, for the colonists, who were a mixture of idlers, incompetent craftsmen, and goldsmiths, had neither the time nor the energy for such upper-class English sports as falconry, upland game shooting, and angling. Of the 114 men who came to Jamestown in April, 1607, only 38 were alive when the next ship arrived the following January. With starvation, malaria, and Indian attacks taking their toll, there was little time for sports.

Despite these hazards, the first game played by white men in America took place in Virginia. It was a game of bowls played on the streets of Jamestown in May, 1611, and Sir Thomas Dale, who viewed the contest as he came ashore, was not at all pleased. Sir Thomas had hastened across the Atlantic in command of a relief ship to save the starving colonists. The sight of the players, who apparently didn't even look up at their savior, so intent were they on the game, nettled Sir Thomas to such an extent that he threatened to put them all in irons. Thus ended the first game recorded in America's history of sports.

Up in New England a few years after the Jamestown bowling incident, Governor William Bradford, of the Plymouth Colony, spoke out against sports with the vigor of Sir Thomas Dale. On Christmas Day, 1621, the Governor saw men "in ye streete at play, openly; some pitching ye barr, & some at stoole ball, and shuch like sports." (Bar pitching was akin to javelin throwing; stool ball was primitive cricket.) The Governor promptly broke up the games and told the players that "ther should be no gameing or revelling in ye streets."

The two pictures above illustrate the Puritans' views on sports. Here (1628) Miles Standish cuts down a maypole erected by Thomas Morton at Merry Mount, near Quincey, Mass. Morton was jugged in the King's name for sponsoring the revels, which consisted of daylight dancing and some imbibing.

On the left, a proclamation against horse racing issued by Boston's Councilmen in 1677. The Puritans' anti-sport attitude had no effect on the neighboring Dutch and English colonists of New Amsterdam.

The picture above shows the Dutch settlers at their favorite sport on the Bowling Green, New Amsterdam. Today the area is surrounded by skyscrapers, but the little park still preserves its original name.

Not so gentle was the Dutch-imported sport of gander pulling (below). If a man pulled off the bird's head while passing in the swift current, he was given the gander. If he failed, he got a ducking.

The first reference to golf in America was made in 1657 when a complaint was issued by the sheriff of Fort Orange (Albany, N. Y.) against three men charged with playing *kolven* on a Sunday. Two years later the Fort Orange magistrates forbid its playing along the streets because it damaged the windows of the houses and exposed the people to injury. The game of *kolven* (left) was not golf as we know it today but it may have been a rudimentary form of the modern game. And it may have been a kind of ice-hockey or field-hockey. No one knows since no description of the game has come down. But it is certain that the Dutch lads enjoyed whacking a ball around in a game they called *kolven* which some scholars translate as golf.

America's first sports trophy was this porringer (below) which is now on display at the Yale University Art gallery. Hand wrought by Pieter van Inburg, it is the oldest piece of silver of American manufacture. The trophy was given to the winner of the 1668 horse race at New Market (Hempstead), Long Island, which was the first race course on the continent.

America's first organized sport was horse racing. It began in 1665, a year after Richard Nicolls took office as first Governor of New York, following the Dutch surrender. Governor Nicolls established the Long Island course, instituted rules of racing, and offered prizes to the winners. He said at the time—as it is still said by horsemen—that his purpose was to improve the breed of horses. In any event, he brought some order to American sport, which, before his time, consisted of unorganized pastimes and recreations.

9

The seal of the Schuylkill Fishing Company (left) is notable in that it represents the oldest club of sportsmen in America. Founded in 1722 at Philadelphia, it is still in existence. The club was a social as well as a sporting organization. The Schuylkill was the first of hundreds of angling clubs. Today, with more than thirty million fishermen in the United States, angling is probably the greatest participant sport in the country.

From the time cricket was introduced in the United States, in the middle of the eighteenth century, until the rise of baseball, nearly a hundred years later, it was one of the most popular games in America. In 1751, teams representing New York and London held a match here in what was probably the first international contest played by an American team. The game spread wherever Englishmen went in this country—along the Eastern seaboard and as far west as Kentucky and Illinois by 1819. Chicago had three cricket teams in 1840. But cricket's leisurely pace was not suited to the American tempo, and it gave way to the far livelier game of baseball.

In contrast to the gentle sports described on the opposite page was a method of fighting common in frontier America, known as gouging. A bare-knuckle fight was as mild as a church supper compared to this brutal sport—if it can be called a sport. In gouging brawls, anything went. Kicking, biting, and kneeing were allowed, and the gouging itself, performed by grabbing the hair near the temple and scooping the eye out of the socket with the thumb nail, was the ultimate aim—like a K.O. in modern boxing.

Gougers used to let their thumb nails grow long for that purpose. The sport was brought here from England, and found favor in the Southern states. It then spread westward to the Ohio Valley, where it seems to have reached its zenith by about 1800. When gouging was in flower, it was not uncommon to see a man minus an eye or an ear or with the tip of his nose missing. The sport was eventually outlawed in all the states. The picture below is from an illustrated book on the technique of rough-and-tumble battling.

Animal baiting (above) and skittles (below) were popular sports associated with the taverns of Colonial America. This picture shows an informal set-to outside a tavern, but more often an enclosure was made with a fence surrounding it beyond which sat several hundred spectators. Then the animal, usually a bull or a bear, was tethered to a ring fastened to the ground, and six or eight dogs were let loose. The battle ended when all the dogs were killed or the animal torn to shreds and brought down. The sport flourished until about 1830.

The ancient sport of cockfighting was introduced from England as early as 1650 and has persisted to this day, although it is legal only in the state of Florida. During the Colonial period, it was practiced everywhere—under cover in New England, winked at but regarded as improper in New York, and publicly conducted throughout the South. From Maryland to New Orleans, the sport was the most popular of all, especially among plantation owners. Matches, or "mains," were held with regularity, and newspapers advertised the time and place of forthcoming battles.

Elkanah Watson, a New England merchant, described a Virginia main held in 1787: "Exceedingly beautiful cocks were produced, armed with long, steel-pointed gaffles which were attached to their natural spurs. The moment the birds were dropped bets ran high. The little heroes appeared trained to the business. . . . They flew upon each other with a rude shock, the cruel gaffles being driven into their bodies and at times directly through their heads. Frequently one, or both, would be struck dead at the first blow. I soon sickened at this barbarous sport."

A terrible game of lacrosse was played on June 4, 1763, at Fort Michillimackinac—terrible not for the brand of play but because it ended in a massacre. The fort stood on what is now Mackinaw City, Michigan, and was garrisoned by English troops. A large number of Ojibway and Sac Indians came to the fort and invited the troops inside to come out and see a lacrosse game between the two nations. Soon the fort was half deserted, the gates left wide open as the unsuspecting soldiers drifted outside. The game began, and the plain in front was covered with a multitude of yelling Indians. Suddenly the ball soared into the air and fell near the gates. The warriors pursued the ball, then dropped their lacrosse bats and snatched hatchets from squaws standing on the sidelines, who had concealed the weapons beneath their blankets. In a moment the shrill cries of the ball players were changed to ferocious war whoops as they hacked at the unarmed soldiers. The Indians rushed the fort and burned it to the ground. There were only two or three survivors of the most terrible lacrosse game ever played.

When George Washington (shown above during a fox hunt) was not at war or at the helm of his country, he lived the life of a typical Southern planter. He was a noted sportsman and outdoorsman, and his favorite sport was fox hunting. In his diary he mentions that he rode to hounds during January and February of 1769 fifteen times, including six successive days in one week. Attired in a sporting costume of blue coat, scarlet waistcoat, and buckskin breeches, Washington had his own pack of hounds and specially trained horses. Fox hunting in Colonial times was confined to a few districts, largely from Philadelphia south to the Carolinas. It was a more rugged sport here than it was in England, although the Southern planters tried to imitate the English gentry. The terrain here was rougher, full of swamps and thick woods, which made the going slow compared to the much faster pace permitted by the open fields of the English countryside. The sport was followed with intense devotion by all the prominent land owners of the upper South.

Fencing, in preparation for the far more serious business of duels "to avenge honor," was practiced by the bloods of pre-Revolutionary America.

To be let to Mares this Season.

At Mr. Philip Platt's on Long-Island, Queen's County, and State of New-York, within about fifteen miles of the City of New-York, and within about three or four miles of the town of Jamaica, and in the neighbourhood of the Township of Newton and Flushing, At FIVE POUNDS the Season for each Mare, the Money to be paid by first of September next.

Any Person wishing to bargain for a Sure Colt, will be treated with at the abovementioned place on reasonable Terms, as he has proved himself a noted Sure Foal getter, where he has formerly stood, in New-Jersey and Pennsylvania.

The Full Blooded Horse

Messenger.

Imported in May, 1788.

MESSENGER is a Grey, full fifteen hands three inches high. He was bred by John Pratt, E. of New-Market, and was got by Membrino, who covered at twenty-five guineas a mare, in 1784. Membrino was got by Engineer, who was got by Sampson, who was the sire of Big Malton, and several other capital racers. His Dam by Turf; his Grand-dam Regulus. This mare was sister to Figerant, and was the dam of Leviathan, a capital racer

MESSENGER won the following Sons in the years 1783, 1784, and 1785, as may be seen by the Racing Calendar

	Guineas
In September, 1783, he beat at Newmarket Mr. Power Colchester, by Shark,	100
Also Mr. Stanley's Horse brother to Sprightley,	30
October 30, 1783, he beat Mr. Napper's Horse Spectre, across the Flat,	300
And Mr. Fox's Horse Pyrrhus, across the New Flat,	300
May, 1784, he beat Lord Barrington's Trigger	150
July, 1784, he beat Mr. Windham's Horse Apothecary,	25
Lord Foley's Rodney, Mr. Wessell's Snowdrop, and Mr. Clark's Flamet,	200
And Lord Foley's Ulyffes,	60
March, 1785, he beat his Royal Highness the Prince of Wales Horse Ulyffes,	100
Also, Mr. Windham's Horse Fortitude,	200
April, 1785, he beat Lord Sherborne's Horse Taylor,	300
	50
	1,515

N. B. In addition to the above, he has won the Kings Plate, and which is the only Horse on the Continent said to have done the same.

Pasture to be had in the Neighbourhood on reasonable Terms.

The arrival of the gray stallion, Messenger, to these shores in 1788 was a momentous event in the history of the American horse, for on the foundation of his blood, a new breed of horses was developed, and a new and completely American sport was built. The sport is harness racing, or trotting, and its founder was Messenger, a thoroughbred who had had a brilliant career as a racing horse on the English turf. He was never a trotter, nor was he imported to breed trotters. Like other blooded English horses which had preceded him, the first being Bulle Rock in 1730, Messenger was brought here to sire runners. But breeders soon found to their amazement that there was in his blood an inheritance factor which favored the trotting gait. From Messenger's sons and daughters came the fastest, most durable, and most perfectly gaited trotters in the world. The gray stallion sired racers as well as trotters, but it was of the latter breed of horses, unique to America, that he was the fountainhead.

The first picture of a football game on American soil (below) is dated 1806 and shows a group of Yale students kicking the ball in front of the college buildings. On the sidewalk, in an academic gown and beaver hat, is Yale president Timothy Dwight (portrait on the right), a stern disciplinarian, who was probably watching the game more to detect any action that would be injurious to morals than as a football fan. The puritanical Dwight disapproved of the theater, horse racing, and almost any pleasure that did not improve the immortal soul. Football, however, was played at Yale thirty years before Dwight took office in 1795, and it was there that the modern game was founded. In his day the game was played with little organization or system. Scrimmage or running with the ball was not allowed, but players could handle the ball to kick it. The ball was usually a leather covered bladder or a leather bag filled with sawdust. From this primitive pastime developed today's number-one college sport, and it is fitting that the first picture of the game should be of the institution which founded it.

17

America's first heavyweight champion was Tom Molineaux, a Virginia slave. He made a name for himself as one of the best slave-boxers in the South when it was the custom for plantation owners to pit their best slaves against each other in ring battles for high stakes. In gratitude, Molineaux's master gave him his freedom, and the fighter came North, where he ran up a string of victories along New York's waterfront. There were no recognized champions in those days, but there's no doubt but what the stocky 185-pound Negro was the best fighting man in America. Having whipped all comers here, Molineaux went to England to have a go at Tom Cribb, one of England's greatest champions.

Molineaux worked his way across on a sailing vessel and was met in Bristol by Bill Richmond, a Negro of American birth who had been brought to England by British officers following the Revolution. Richmond took Molineaux under his wing and got him two fights which the ex-slave won handily. Then, on December 10, 1810, came his match with Tom Cribb (right) for 200 guineas and the championship belt.

Molineaux was the better man that day. He had Cribb licked but was bilked out of the victory by the trickery of the Englishman's seconds. The Negro was in front all the way, and, at the end of the twenty-third round, Cribb was so far gone that he couldn't come to scratch. The referee should have given the fight to Molineaux right then but instead he listened to Cribb's handlers, who claimed that the Negro had leaden weights hidden in his fists. In the wrangling which lasted several minutes, Cribb recovered, and Molineaux, unused to the raw British clime, suffered a chill. The tide of battle turned after that, and Cribb won in the fortieth round. They fought again the next year, and this time Cribb won against a badly conditioned Molineaux, who had taken to rum. But the first battle should have gone to the Negro. Even the English sports admitted that.

Fig. 1.

John.

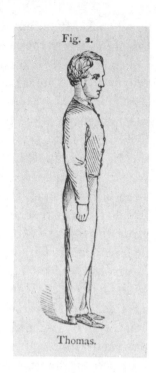

Fig. 2.

Thomas.

The German system of gymnastics had a great vogue in this country following the establishment of the first U.S. gymnasium at Northampton, Mass., in 1825 by Charles Beck who was a disciple of Friedrich Jahn, founder of the first "turnplatz" in Germany. The pictures of the above two lads illustrate the benefits of the gym. John, with drooping head, evidently spurned the flying rings. Not so Thomas whose sturdy body was developed by the German technique of physical training.

The high and low in contemporary sports is illustrated on this page—the proper and sedate young archers of Philadelphia (above), and a group of rustics outside a tavern betting on a turkey race (right), the winner being the first bird to get across the bridge.

In 1828, America's first archery club was formed as the United Bowmen of Philadelphia, a select group of twenty-five gentlemen, who adopted a natty uniform of light-blue jackets and white trousers. The purpose of the club was to encourage the ancient sport and engage in healthful recreation. It must have been healthful, for one of the club's regulations firmly stated that nothing but water could be drunk at its meetings. Until the club disbanded in 1859, it held annual tournaments and awarded silver trophies. It was the forerunner of the National Archery Association, a country-wide organization whose membership today numbers thousands of enthusiasts.

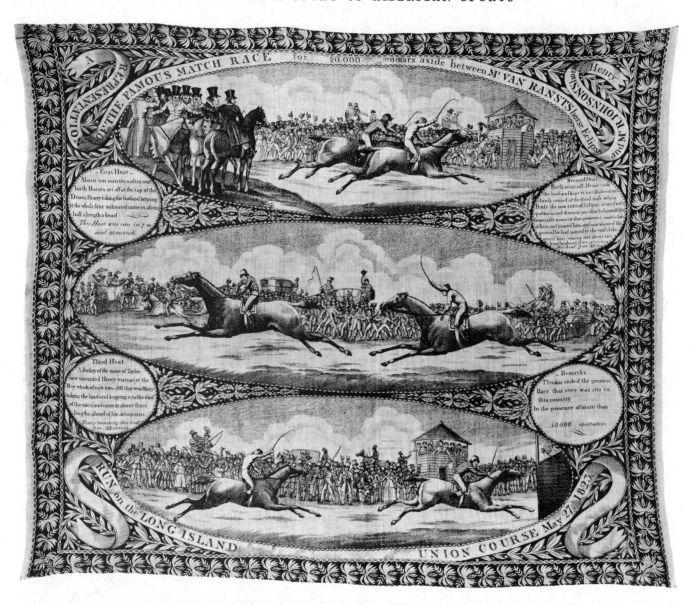

A horse race was responsible for the first great crowd to witness a sporting event in America. It took place on the last Tuesday in May, 1823, when an estimated 100,000 people stormed the Union Race Course on Long Island to see a match race between Eclipse, the Northern champion, and Sir Henry, the fastest thoroughbred in the South. It was the North against the South, a matter of sectional pride and intense rivalry. For weeks the match had created nation-wide excitement, and visitors came from all over the country to see it. The conditions of the race were the best two out of three four-mile heats for $20,000 a side over the mile-long course. A tap of the drums started the horses off. When Sir Henry won the first heat, the Southerners, who had bet heavily on him, were unable to contain themselves. But their joy was short-lived, for Eclipse won the next two heats and all the money. This was the first of a series of intersectional races but none of the subsequent ones drew as great a crowd. The country had never been more aroused over any contest, political or sporting, than it was by the great match between Eclipse and Sir Henry.

America's most beloved sports figure was Hiram Woodruff, the country's master reinsman during the middle of the last century. His career is the story of American trotting from 1833, when, as a boy of sixteen, he first trotted under saddle, until 1865, when he retired as a sulky driver. A spare, sinewy 150-pounder, Woodruff could get things out of a horse that no one else could. People who bet against him at country fairs used to say, "It's 20 to 30 per cent in favor of any horse Hiram Woodruff drives." Few bet against him. He was more than a clever driver, however. He was sincerely interested in improving the breed of horses and devoted much of his life to that purpose. Of unquestioned honesty, Hiram was the hero of rural America.

Professional foot races and walking contests were common sporting events in the last century, especially foot races. The runners of the day were called pedestrians, or "peds." The picture on the left shows the great international ten-mile race which took place at Hoboken, New Jersey, on November 19, 1844, for a purse of $700 to the winner. A crowd of 25,000 was on hand to see the English peds, John Barlow and Tom Greenhalgh, go against America's best. So dense was the crowd that a dozen men on horseback had to precede the runners to keep the track clear. Barlow won in 54 minutes, 10 seconds. This race was typical of the many staged during the 1830–1870 period when professional foot racing was in vogue on both sides of the Atlantic.

Below is a cartoon of an international walking race between athletes representing America, England, and Ireland. These toe-and-heel contests became popular after the peds had had their day.

One of the country's fleetest peds in the 1840's was this bewhiskered Mercury, who was known as The American Deer. He was William Jackson, a ten-miler who burned up the tracks both here and in England. The peds were a colorful lot in those days. Each wore his own colors as jockeys do today. For example, Pat Mahoney, the running butcher, wore a green shirt, blue breeches, and white stockings; George Clammer, a carpenter, wore a suit of white silk with red belt and pink slippers; and the Seneca Indian, Deerfoot, was clad in breechclout and moccasins, and wore a colored feather in his hair. Besides these distance runners there were sprinters, a notable one being George Steward, who, in 1847, was credited with running 120 yards in 11½ seconds and 200 yards in 19½ seconds. Amateur track and field sports came into being with the formation of the New York Athletic Club in 1868. With other amateur clubs following in the larger cities, professional foot racing soon became a thing of the past.

When the schooner *America* left Boston Harbor (above) in June, 1851, to sail against England's best, there were few who thought she had a chance. The Royal Yacht Squadron of England was the oldest yacht club in the world, and its skippers the most skillful. But the *America* surprised the world by defeating fourteen picked British vessels, which had no restrictions on tonnage or rig, in the difficult sixty-mile course around the Isle of Wight. The special cup won by the *America* immediately became known as "The America's Cup" and is so known today.

England tried to lift the cup in 1870 by sending the challenger *Cambria* to these waters, but the result was a sad one for John Bull, as this cartoon indicates.

Commodore John C. Stevens, a wealthy financier from Hoboken, skippered the *America* to her triumph in British waters. An enthusiastic yachtsman all his life, the Commodore was the most noted sports patron of his time. It was he who arranged the great Eclipse–Sir Henry match race in 1823, and he backed the Northern horse to the limit. A few years later, over the same Union Race Course, he made a sizeable wager that he could produce a man who could run ten miles in an hour. Stevens won the bet when Henry Stannard, a farmer-ped, covered the distance in 59 minutes and 44 seconds. Whenever there was an outstanding sports event in the mid-1800's, the Commodore usually had a hand in it.

Perhaps the high point in the Commodore's career was the honor paid him by Queen Victoria (below) when she came aboard the *America* to congratulate him on his victory over the British racing yachts.

Winslow Homer, the American artist, drew the above picture of a Harvard football match in 1857. The game then was no longer the mild pastime it had been in Timothy Dwight's day. At Harvard and Yale it had degenerated into a class rush, a mass assault between freshmen and sophomores. The ball was merely an excuse for mayhem. This picture shows the kick-off, with the sophomores lined up on the right, while the hesitating freshmen advance toward the ball. As soon as the ball was touched it was forgotten in the general riot that followed. "Boys and young men knocked each other down, tore off each other's clothing. Eyes were bunged, faces blackened and bloodied, and shirts and coats torn to rags," said the *New York Evening Post* in describing a Yale inter-class struggle. The game got so out of hand that it was banned at both colleges in 1860.

In England (right), a similar type of football was played by villagers in the streets. But it had become a regulated game in the English public schools years before it was outlawed at Harvard and Yale.

Billiards was a popular tavern pastime from early colonial days. Many people frowned upon it, however. One disapprover was John Adams, who said that "the billiard table" was for "rakes and fools."

The game reached full growth when the first match for the billiard championship of the United States was held on April 12, 1859, at Fireman's Hall in Detroit. This picture shows the two contestants, Michael J. Phelan and John Seereiter, playing before a genteel audience, which numbered several ladies. It would be interesting to know how many ladies were there at the finish, for the match lasted from 7:30 P.M. until 5 o'clock the next morning. The terms of the match were a $5,000 side bet, plus $5,000 put up by the promoter, and a portion of the gate, the winner to take all. Seereiter had a high run of 197, but steady Mike Phelan took the match by 96 points and walked off with a purse of $15,000. The game then was a mixture of modern billiards and pocket billiards. The table had six pockets, four balls were used, and points were earned by caroms and by pocketing the balls. Phelan, the first professional champion, wrote textbooks on the game and was its foremost figure until he retired in 1870.

THE GREAT INTERNATIONAL PRIZEFIGHT
FOR THE CHAMPIONSHIP OF THE WORLD

John C. Heenan

Tom Sayers

The first boxing match to stir public interest to a high pitch on both sides of the Atlantic was the battle between John C. Heenan, the American champion, and Tom Sayers, king of the English bareknucklers. Never before had a fight attracted such a distinguished gathering. In the crowd, according to reports, were such luminaries as the Prince Consort, William Makepeace Thackeray, Thomas Nast, the American cartoonist, and members of the nobility and Parliament. Scores of American sportsmen who had sailed with Heenan were at the ringside. American newspapers and weeklies sent reporters and artists to give a first-hand account. The British press was fully represented. In all, some 2,500 people were on the scene at Farnborough, near London, where the battle took place on April 17, 1860.

Heenan (right), the Benicia Boy, so called because he lived in the California town of that name, acquired the U.S. championship upon the retirement of the reigning titleholder, John Morrissey, in 1860. He stood six feet two, weighed 195 and was perfectly proportioned. A clever boxer and hard puncher, the Benicia Boy delighted the British with his unassuming manner. They called him "The Immense Invader."

Little Tom Sayers was the marvel of his day. A middleweight, he never weighed more than 155 pounds but he was fast, brainy, elusive and game. He beat bigger men with ease. Sayers would have done well in any period of ring history. He was so idolized by the British sporting world that they made him the 1 to 2 betting favorite over Heenan even though he was outweighed by 40 pounds and at 34 was nine years older than the Benicia Boy.

It was to be a fight to the finish for $1,000 a side (winner-take-all) and the championship belt.

A bare-knuckle fight under the London Prize Ring Rules was more or less a supervised street fight—a combination of boxing and wrestling. A round ended only when a man went down, by being either knocked down or hurled to the turf. A round, therefore, could last but a few seconds or it might go over twenty minutes. As soon as a man went down, the referee called, "Time!" and the fallen fighter was dragged to his corner, where his handlers attended him, as shown below. At the end of thirty seconds, the referee, who stood outside the ring, began counting aloud. Within eight seconds the fighters had to leave their corners unaided and advance to a mark, or scratch, drawn on the turf in the center of the ring. (Hence the expressions "toe the mark" and "come to scratch.") If a man failed to come to scratch in eight seconds after the thirty-second respite, he was declared the loser. There was no butting or gouging allowed, no hitting below the belt or seizing a man in a wrestling hold below the waist. Outside of that, almost anything went.

Just before time was called, the seconds and bottle-holders of the fighters came to the center of the ring and shook hands all around.

It was half-past seven in the morning when the fighters came to the mark and shook hands. "We have a nice day for our business," Sayers smiled, noting the cloudless skies. Heenan grinned, time was called, and the battle was on. The crowd roared as the Englishman drew first blood with a sharp left to the Benicia Boy's nose. (The gamblers always bet on first blood and first knockdown.) The big American rushed his man constantly, using his superior strength and weight to good advantage. He scored clean knockdowns to end the second, third, fourth, and fifth rounds. But the ringwise Briton kept jabbing and moving away, kept pecking at Heenan's eyes. At the end of the seventh the American's right eye was completely closed. It was in this round that Sayers ruptured a tendon in his right arm, rendering it useless for hitting. He could still use his left, though, and did so with great effect. Heenan, always smiling, always the aggressor, kept flooring his man.

The American was not knocked down once and came to scratch first every time. Both men were bathed in blood, but still they fought on. Now it was a question of whether Sayers could last long enough to close both of Heenan's eyes and force him to quit. Everybody saw that it was his only chance. In the thirty-seventh round, Heenan got Sayers in a headlock and was strangling and hammering him into insensibility when the Englishman's supporters broke into the ring to save him. The referee called it a draw, but it was clear that Heenan would have won had the battle gone on. It lasted two hours and twenty minutes. Championship belts were awarded to both men and each was acclaimed as champion—Sayers in England, Heenan in America. Which one was the *real* champion did not matter. Sayers never fought again. Heenan fought but once more and lost to Tom King.

Around the end of the eighteenth century, school-boys along the Eastern seaboard began playing bat-and-ball games of various styles, according to the number of players involved. One of the earliest of these games, one-old-cat, was simplicity itself. Only one base and three players were required: pitcher, catcher, and batter. With more players, the game needed more bases and it became two-old-cat, three-old-cat, and so on. When there were enough players to form sides, it was called rounders, town ball, goal ball, or base ball, depending upon where it was played. Whatever the name, the games had one thing in common: the batter hit the ball and ran for a goal, or base, while the fielders tried to put him out by catching the ball on the fly or by fielding it and touching him with it before he got to a base.

The British game of rounders, which is still played by boys and girls in England, is the ancestor of our national game. In this country, rounders became known as "town ball" because village lads used to play it on New England greens at the time of town meetings. It was a pick-up game with any number of players on a side. Rules were few and elastic; equipment was simple, consisting usually of a stout stick for a bat and a ball of tightly wound string without a covering. There were no written rules of play at first; it was a community recreation rather than an organized sport. But when college students and grown men took it up in the 1830's, it developed into a game that required more skill. Of the many names it had—rounders, town ball, base ball—it was "base ball" that finally won out.

PLAYING BALL

Cricket and baseball were equally popular in America before the Civil War, and for many years it was a question as to which would become our national game. Baseball fans ridiculed the English game, as the above cartoon indicates. To them it was a slow, silly pastime for over-aged men, a typical player being this John Bull-like character. Actually, the game requires a great deal of skill and physical activity, even though it often takes a couple of days to finish a game, with time out for tea.

Baseball on Boston Common, 1834.

This woodcut of boys playing ball on Boston Common appeared in *The Book of Sports*, by Robin Carver (1834). The book is a milestone in baseball history, for it contains the first printed rules of the game and the first picture of a baseball contest.

Carver's rules for the game he called "base ball" are basically similar to the modern ones: the batter was out after three strikes or a caught fly; when he got a hit, he tried to circle the bases and score a run; the infield was diamond-shaped and there were four bases; the base where the batter stood was called "home." The boys in 1834, however, ran clockwise; first base was where third is now. Carver's "base ball" rules were copied word for word from an earlier book published in England, in which the game was called "rounders." In the beginning, then, the two games were identical, differing only in name.

Even when baseball was taken up by men and was no longer exclusively a boy's pastime, the pitcher (lower left) was required to serve the ball underhand with unbent elbow. His purpose was not to fool the batter but to give him what he wanted.

The plaque on the left marks the site of the beginning of organized baseball. And the photograph above is the first picture of a baseball team ever made. Taken in 1857, it shows the members of the New York Knickerbockers, a baseball club that came into existence a number of years before that time. The early Knicks were a group of gentlemanly amateurs who first met on a vacant lot in lower Manhattan on Sunday afternoons in 1842 for "health, recreation and social enjoyment," and, incidentally, to play baseball. Their games were informal, gentle affairs between teams composed of members only, not against some of the other baseball clubs which were being formed in New York at that time. The Knicks kept to themselves until the historic day, June 19, 1846, when they took on another amateur team, known as the New York Club, at the Elysian Fields, a summer resort across the river in Hoboken. This was the first match game ever played, the first between two ball clubs. The Knicks, playing under their own rules, which they had adopted a year before, got slaughtered, 24 to 1. But the game was a great stride forward in the development of the sport. The Knick's rules called for nine men on a side; flat bases; three out, all out; and, most important, a diamond with the bases ninety feet apart. For the first time, baseball was played as we know it today.

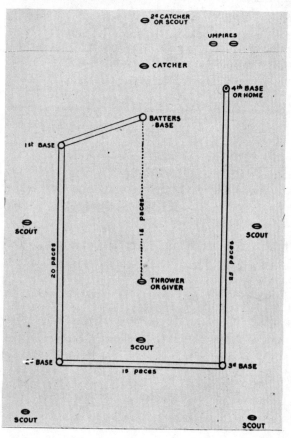

The above photostat of Page 1 of the Knickerbocker Club's Game Book is the first box score of a baseball game, an account of the June 19, 1846, match against the New Yorks. One of the players, named Davis, should be enshrined in Cooperstown's Baseball Hall of Fame, for a notation in the book states that the umpire was forced to fine him six cents for swearing. The original Game Book, with every game neatly recorded, is on view today at the New York Public Library.

The strange-looking playing field pictured at left was used throughout New England many years after the Knicks had adopted the regulation diamond. The New England Game, as it was called, differed greatly from the New York Game, as did the Philadelphia version of baseball. When the Knicks drew up their first set of rules in 1845, they intended them for Knickerbockers only. No one ever dreamed that the New York rules would one day be accepted by baseball clubs everywhere.

40

A STINGER.

ALEXANDER JOY CARTWRIGHT, Jr.
"FATHER OF MODERN BASE BALL."
SET BASES 90 FEET APART.
ESTABLISHED 9 INNINGS AS GAME
AND 9 PLAYERS AS TEAM. ORGANIZED
THE KNICKERBOCKER BASEBALL CLUB
OF N.Y. IN 1845. CARRIED BASEBALL
TO PACIFIC COAST AND HAWAII
IN PIONEER DAYS.

In the New England game, a base runner could be put out by being hit with a thrown ball while he was on the base paths. This was called plugging, or soaking, a feature that persisted in New England until the Civil War. The Knicks were the first to take this play out of the game by stating in their rule book that a man is out "if the ball is in the hands of an adversary on the base . . . it being understood that in no instance is a ball to be thrown at him." In New York, then, when a ball was fielded it was thrown *to* a baseman, not *at* a base runner. This put the game out of the rounders class.

Alexander J. Cartwright is to be thanked for that rule, for it was he who drew up the first set of rules when he organized the Knickerbocker Base Ball Club. He is also credited with setting the bases ninety feet apart. A surveyor, Cartwright figured that at ninety feet a grounder handled cleanly by an infielder and thrown to first should beat the runner by a fraction of a second. It proved to be the perfect distance. In more than a century of play, baseball has seen many changes in equipment—in the bat, the ball, and the gloves, but ninety feet is still the perfect distance in the race between the runner and a ball thrown to a base.

AMHERST EXPRESS.
EXTRA.
WILLIAMS AND AMHERST
BASE BALL AND CHESS!
MUSCLE AND MIND!!
July 1st and 2d, 1859.

THE ORIGIN OF THE MATCH.
At the commencement of this term, it was privately proposed among the Amherst students to challenge Williams College to a game of Ball. In the second or third week the challenge was given by the committee of the College. Notice had been privately sent to Williams of this intention, that both parties might have equal opportunity of practice. The challenge was readily accepted, and in turn Williams challenged to a game at Chess, that there might be "a trial of mind as well as muscle". This being at once agreed upon,

state this, to correct reports to the contrary. Williams appeared in the uniform of club belts, Amherst decidedly in undress. In size and muscular development, we thought Amherst, on the whole, superior.; while in agility, in running and leaping, the Williams boys excelled. By some ridiculous mistake a report was spread that the thrower from Amherst was the professional blacksmith of the place, hired for the occasion. This rumor afforded great amusement to that very fine player, and his comrades. A bystander remarked that the story seemed probable for

A. J. Quick, S. W. Pratt, J. H. Knox, J. E. Bush, R. E. Beecher, H. F. C. Nichols, (umpire, C. R. Taft.)
Referee.—W. R. Plunkett, Esq., President of the Pittsfield Base Ball Club.

SYNOPSIS OF THE GAME.
Amherst held the first inning by lot, and Williams played the last by turn. Williams played best at first, making ten tallies to Amherst's one ; when the latter went in to win, and made twenty to their one, and kept the advantage throughout, making more than two tallies for one

considerable delay on a reference to the umpires, Storrs made a home knock, on the front field, fine run for Amherst, making 12 tallies, W. 0.
17th. Gridley caught out by Simmons, (W) Quick caught out by Hyde—tallies 0.
18th. Tomson out on 3d base, (W) Beecher caught out by Claflin, each makes 1 tally.
19th. Storrs out by Fitch, (good catch,) (W) Parker caught out by Claflin—tallies 0.
20th. Cushman caught out by Simmons, (W) Fitch hit by Emmons, 4th base, makes 1

UMPIRE.

The rules originated by the Knickerbockers were adopted by all the amateur clubs in the New York area in the 1850's, and the new game soon spread to the colleges. On July 1, 1859, Amherst and Williams staged the first intercollegiate baseball game, Amherst winning 73 to 32, in a marathon that lasted four hours. The Amherst hurler, named Hyde, went all the way and was so effective in holding the Williamses down to 32 runs that they charged him with being a ringer, a blacksmith in the guise of an Amherst student. If so, he was the game's first ringer. The next day Williams evened things by outwitting Amherst in the chess match which was the climax of the two-day festival of mind and muscle.

Baseball's first star was Jim Creighton, a nineteen-year-old wonder who pitched for the Excelsiors of Brooklyn. The team went on the road in 1860 and beat several upstate New York clubs, then swung south to Philadelphia, Wilmington, and Baltimore. With Creighton hurling, they won fifteen games without a loss. Among their victims was a newly formed team called the Philadelphia Athletics. The Excelsiors were the first team to make a tour. They caused great excitement wherever they played, often drawing crowds of more than 3,000. They were the game's first missionaries. New baseball clubs sprang up in their wake. The Brooklyn Nine did more to make the game our national pastime than any other club up to that time. Creighton was something new to see. Instead of merely serving the ball to the batter, Jim burned it across the plate. He had speed, control, and the rudiments of a curve. Jim changed the character of pitching technique.

George Wright, the game's first outstanding professional, is the earliest player to be enshrined in Baseball's Hall of Fame at Cooperstown. He was the son of a professional English cricketeer who came to this country to bowl for the St. George Cricket Club on Staten Island. Young George soon switched from cricket to baseball. His older brother, Harry, had done the same thing before him, undoubtedly to the old man's disgust. Although he was a professional bowler, Harry was invited in 1856 to join the exclusive Knickerbocker Club, whose members were amateurs of the bluest blood. The Knicks were tired of getting beaten and wanted to win some ball games. Baseball was beginning to change, shifting from an amateur to a semi-pro status. Within a few years the Wright brothers were to make history by forming the first frankly professional baseball team. Harry was the organizer, but George was to become the brilliant performer, the game's first professional star.

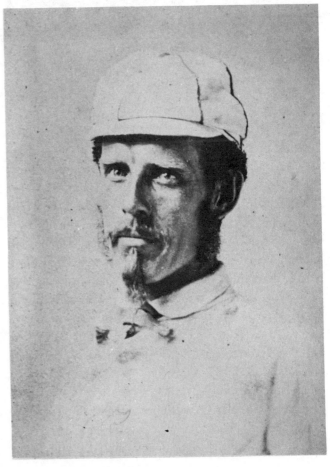

This picture shows Union soldiers playing baseball in the Confederate prison camp at Salisbury, N. C. Note the similarity between this game and today's sand-lot softball. The basemen hugged the sacks, while the catcher stood about ten feet behind the plate and took the pitch on the first bounce; no gloves were used; the bats were thin, and pitching was underhand. The Boys in Blue from New England and New York brought the game South and taught it to their Confederate captors. In Union Army camps, men from the Midwest saw it for the first time and soon learned to play it. After the war, soldiers from both forces took the game home with them and introduced it to the South and Midwest. Its rise in popularity was phenomenal. But even before the Civil War, the game was on its way. To go back a moment: In 1858, twenty-five ball clubs centered around New York met and formed the National Association of Base Ball Players to clarify the rules of the game. (One of the most important rules established the nine-inning game—not 21 runs, which before that time had constituted a full game.) In the next two years, the National Association grew to more than twice its original size, and the old Knicks no longer controlled the game. It was now baseball in the true sense, with a league and a uniform set of rules; yet it is interesting to note what one author in 1864 thought of the game. In an early book on sports, the chapter headed "Base Ball" begins: "This game, *which is Rounders or Town Ball*, bids fair to become our national pastime." There were those in 1864 who still thought of the game as rounders, but it had long since passed that stage.

The Cincinnati Red Stockings, shown below receiving a giant bat from admiring fans after their triumphant tour in 1869, was the first ball club to turn pro. George Ellard, Manager of the amateur Reds, and Harry Wright, the ex-cricketeer, decided that baseball could be made to pay. They signed up a group of amateur stars from New York, Washington, and Brooklyn. It was the first time a team had ever been made up of players other than home-town boys. Harry Wright got Mrs. Bertram, a Cincinnati seamstress, to make the uniforms—knee-length pants and long red stockings. Salaries ranged from $1,400 down to $800. George Wright, playing shortstop, got the top salary, $200 more than brother Harry, who managed the club and played center field. The Wright boys were good, especially George, who was the star of the infield. It was almost impossible to get a "grasscutter" through him. He played barehanded and in spikeless shoes. The ball was hard, too. In his first season he hit 59 homers and batted .518. It was quite a team, in many respects the most remarkable of all time. From May to November, 1869, they played 57 games without a single loss. They met the best clubs in the country on alien diamonds

before hostile crowds. Picked nines in Boston, Pittsburgh, Louisville, St. Louis, San Francisco, and many other cities along the way went down to defeat. They traveled with only nine men, and, except for a few broken fingers, there were no serious casualties. Cincinnati went wild when the Reds came home. The players were met at the station, paraded through the streets, and received by the mayor at City Hall, where they were given the 27-foot long bat. The following season they started off by winning 22 straight. It looked as if they were going on forever, but defeat finally came to them when, on June 14, 1870, they met the Atlantics of Brooklyn. Before 20,000 standees, the Reds dropped a close one, losing 8 to 7 in 11 innings. It was their first beating in 92 games. The Reds were good, not as ludicrous as some of the old photographs make them look. Years later, when gloves and masks came into the game, an old-timer sang of them thusly:

We used no mattress on our hands,
No cage upon our face;
We stood right up and caught the ball
With courage and with grace.

CHAPTER TWO

The Gas-Lit Era 1871–1899

At the end of the Civil War, there were virtually no organized sports in America as we now know them. Consider, for example, the ten most popular spectator sports today, most of which, incidentally, were unknown before Lee's surrender. Based on the number of tickets sold annually, they are, in the order of their popularity: basketball, horse racing, auto racing, baseball, football, boxing, ice hockey, track and field, golf, and tennis. Now let's look at the status of these sports before 1865. Basketball had not been invented. Baseball, in its swaddling clothes, was an amateur sport known to only a handful of players and without national organization. Football was a crude form of soccer. In disgrace at Harvard and Yale, it was played informally by a few schoolboy teams around Boston. Horse racing was the exception. Our oldest organized sport, it had a following since Colonial days, and tracks operated all through the Civil War. Prize fighting, the most disreputable of all sports, was illegal in every state and attracted only thugs and bums. Golf, tennis, ice hockey, and auto racing were unknown. Track and field sports did not come into existence until after the Civil War. The nearest thing to it was professional foot racing, a sport which fell into disrepute because of its crookedness.

The sports fan of less than a century ago had lean pickings. Now and then he could take in a ball game or a horse race and, once in a blue moon, a prize fight, if he was willing to risk getting slugged by some hoodlum or having his pocket picked. There wasn't much for him to look at in those days, and his comfort wasn't considered at the few sporting events

he could attend. There were no stadiums or indoor arenas. He stood on his feet while watching ball games, prize fights, and foot races.

The gas-lit era saw the greatest upsurge of sports in this country's history. From the end of the Civil War until the turn of the century, practically all of our sports were founded and organized. The rise of sports in this period is a phenomenon not easy to explain. It was due, perhaps, to the growth of industry, which meant more leisure time; to the increase in population, especially in cities; and to the decline of puritanism. In other words, more people had more time for sports and no longer felt guilty about enjoying them. At any rate, sports on the grand scale were on the way.

As an example of how sports were developing at that time, one year (1876) saw the formation of the National Baseball League, The Intercollegiate Football Association, and the ICAAAA (intercollegiate track and field). That was a banner year, but the list continues: Rowing Association of American Colleges (1871); U.S. Lawn Tennis Association (1881); American Hockey Association (1887); U.S. Golf Association (1894). Basketball was invented in 1891, and boxing came of age a year later, when the first glove bout for the heavyweight championship was held. Everything was happening in the gas-lit era.

The gentle game of croquet, as played in the Victorian era—not to be compared with roque, its modern version—was the first game played by both men and women in America. It was a social amusement rather than a test of skill. At first it was played on ragged lawns with uneven wooden balls and mallets.

The Park Place Croquet Club of Brooklyn, organized in 1864 with twenty-five members, was the pioneer croquet club. The game became so popular that in 1882 the National Croquet Association was formed to revise and standardize the rules. After that the men took over, and, when the National Roque Association came into being late in the century, the earlier "courting game" was transformed into a game demanding skill and strategy. Roque today bears little resemblance to its gentle ancestor.

The ladies not only began playing games in the gas-lit era; they began to appear at sporting events. On the right, the fair ones take in a dog race, a sport which was introduced here in the 1870's. Greyhound and whippet racing didn't amount to much in this country until 1919, when the mechanical rabbit, an invention of Owen P. Smith of California, appeared. Today the sport's Mecca is Florida, where thirteen tracks operate nightly the year round.

In 1869, when the Cincinnati Red Stockings were touring the country, a strange-looking vehicle, called a velocipede (above), was born on the American stage. The Hanlon brothers, famous acrobats of the time, used the velocipede in their trick riding act. Soon a velocipede craze started. Manufacturers turned out the wooden-framed, iron-shod wheeled vehicles by the hundreds, and velocipede-riding schools opened throughout the east. But the "bone shakers" were heavy, clumsy, and without springs. When the boys took them out on the streets they couldn't handle them the way the Hanlons did. The craze collapsed as quickly as it had bloomed.

The high-wheeler (left) was a different thing. (So was the rider.) Much lighter than the bone shaker, it had a metal framework, steel-wire spokes, and hard rubber tires. A header from the high perch was a menace, however, and women didn't go in for the sport until the drop-frame "safety," with the pneumatic tire, became universal in the '90's.

Ice-boat racing against the crack trains that traveled the Hudson River route was a popular sport among the young bloods of Manhattan in the 1880's. Although the early ice boats were cumbersome compared to the streamlined craft in use today, in any kind of a breeze they would whip the fastest trains and in a stiff breeze could do better than 100 miles an hour.

Another national "rage" which rivaled the bicycling craze of the gas-lit era was roller skating. In the mid-'80's almost every city and small town in the United States had a rink of some sort. The reason for the sudden popularity was the introduction of metal wheels with pin bearings which permitted a skater to roll along smoothly and work up speed. Before that time the rollers were wooden spools, which would often crack and send the skater headlong. The new wheels made skating easier and safer. Women and girls went in for the new recreation, and by 1885, when the vogue reached its peak, more than twenty million dollars were invested in roller-skating properties.

The old sport of gander pulling didn't die out when the Dutch surrendered New Amsterdam. It persisted in backwoods America right up to the end of the nineteenth century. Instead of sitting in a boat (see page 7), the gander puller rode at the bird and tried to twist its head off as he charged by. If he failed, he got spilled for his pains.

Another illegal country sport was cockfighting, which is more popular today than at any time in its history. Once considered a poor man's sport— as indeed it was in the last century, it is now conducted on a grander scale than ever before. The World Series of the sport is the International Cocking Tournament, held annually in Florida, which calls for a $1,000 entry fee and offers purses totalling $40,000 in a solid week of cockfighting.

Another early American sport still practiced today was the turkey shoot (right). The bird was placed about a hundred yards from the shooter, who paid a fee for a chance to knock its head off. If he did, he got the turkey; if he missed, he was out the price of his shot.

Still another back-country sport was ratting, which was a part of tavern life throughout the last century. In preparation for the event, several rats were trapped alive. Then, when the match came off, they were released in a pit with a dog or a weasel, and the slaughter was on. It wasn't a question of who would win; the rats were always killed. It was a matter of how long it would take the animal to finish them up. Bets were made on the basis of time. Rattings are still staged in this country, but so rarely that the sport is virtually nonexistent.

EDWARD P. WESTON.

It is difficult in this day and age to believe that heel-and-toe walking races were once so popular that crowds used to jam Gilmore's Garden (the forerunner of Madison Square Garden) to watch men plod along for hours in an unnatural gait. Walking events are still on the Olympic program, and the 3,000-meter walk is held annually in the National A.A.U. Track and Field Championship Meet, but they have long since been dropped as an intercollegiate event. In the eyes of most modern sports fans, there is something ridiculous about seeing a group of men straining every muscle to get ahead without being able to use what nature gave them to do so. But fans in the '70's and '80's didn't feel that way.

The greatest long-distance walker of the era was Edward Payson Weston (left), who began his career in 1861, at the age of 22, when he made a bet that he could walk from Boston to Washington, a distance of 478 miles, in ten consecutive days in order to reach Washington in time to see Lincoln inaugurated. Weston made it just as the inauguration ceremonies were ending.

Before Weston's time, all the great walkers were Englishmen. They excelled at road walking (right), and the best hikers averaged more than 50 miles a day in a two-week marathon of continuous walking.

Weston outdid the Britishers at their own game. On the open road, at distances of four- or five-hundred miles and upwards, he had no equal. Below he is shown in a six-day go-as-you-please race held in Gilmore's Garden. In these contests, a man could walk any time, night or day, and rest whenever he chose, the winner being the one who had covered the greatest distance at the end of six days. Weston won $10,000 in 1867 by walking from Portland, Maine, to Chicago in 26 days. Perhaps his most remarkable feat was his 105-day hike from New York to San Francisco in celebration of his seventieth birthday.

International rifle-shooting got under way in 1874 when an eight-man Irish team came to this country to shoot it out with America's best on the Creedmoor, Long Island, range. The Irishmen had beaten England the year before and were looking for new worlds to conquer. The American team, representing the newly formed (1871) National Rifle Association, under the leadership of General George W. Wingate (second row, center, in the above picture of the Yankee team), was untested. The match was for a stake of $500, each man to shoot seven times at each range, 800, 900, and 1,000 yards. The Americans used breechloading rifles; the Irish, muzzleloaders. More than five thousand people were on hand to see the day-long contest held on September 26. They were rewarded with a dramatic finale when Colonel John Bodine, the American anchor man, squeezed off his last shot. The match was so close that if he hit the target America would win by one point; if he missed, Ireland would win. The Colonel sent his bullet into the white disk for a four point bullseye and America won 934 to 931.

This cartoon by Thomas Nast (right) appeared in *Harper's Weekly* in 1874, showing the not very friendly looking ladies, Columbia and Eire, shaking hands.

The following year the American team went to England and defeated the British riflemen at Wimbledon. They brought back a silver tankard (the Wimbledon Cup) which was presented to them by Princess Elizabeth, the daughter of Queen Victoria.

In America's Centennial Year, 1876, this country played host to rifle teams from Ireland, Scotland, England, Australia and Canada at an international match staged at Creedmoor. Again the Americans were victorious, this time by 22 points over the Irish team. Below, Sir Henry Halford of the British team takes his first shot on the Creedmoor range.

The pictures on these two pages show scenes typical of horse racing in the gas-lit era, when the sport found new life.

Above, the paddock, with bettors and bookies exchanging slips while an owner gives instructions to a diminutive jockey.

Opposite, right, ladies and dudes watch the races from the members' stand, while below is an early Kentucky Derby. Note the long stirrups and English-style seat, which was universal until American jockeys introduced the "monkey crouch" in the '90's.

When the Civil War broke out, racing came to a standstill in the South, except at Lexington, Kentucky, where regular meetings were held all through the War, save for the fall of 1862. Southerners were forced to sell their horses to the Confederate Government, and many of their finest thoroughbreds were lost in cavalry charges.

In the North, many tracks kept running as usual. John Morrissey, gambler, former bare-knuckle champion and Tammany politician, built a race track at Saratoga Springs, New York, and opened it on August 3, 1863. Morrissey persuaded socialites William R. Travers and Leonard W. Jerome, grandfather of Winston Churchill, to go in with him on the venture. It was such a success that Travers and Jerome built their own track near New York three years later. This was the beginning of a period of tremendous prosperity in racing. Tracks opened in Chicago, Cincinnati, Springfield, Baltimore, Boston, and on the Pacific Coast. Even the threadbare South responded by building courses in Memphis, Louisville, and New Orleans, and around New York City three new tracks were built before 1875.

Churchill Downs in Louisville (right) was just another one among the many tracks built at the time, and when, in 1875, the first Kentucky Derby was run, netting the owner of the winning colt, Aristides, $2,850, no one thought that it would one day become the most highly prized and traditional race in America.

ON THE MEMBER'S STAND

The belle of the gas-lit era was a slight doe-like bay horse named Goldsmith Maid (shown above crossing the finish line in front). The Maid is in many respects the most remarkable horse ever bred in this country. On the New Jersey farm where she was reared, she was so fiery that she kicked several buggies to bits before she could be broken to harness. It took three years to teach her to trot, and she was eight before she ran her first race. She won it easily against experienced horses. Then began a career which took her across the country several times to meet the fastest trotters in the land. For years she was invincible. She ended her career with a record of 350 winning heats and total earnings of $364,200. Yet she never won as much as $5,000 in a single race. The Maid was ageless, and her speed increased as she grew older. At 14 she stepped the mile for a new record of 2 minutes and 17 seconds. (She drew only the cumbersome high-wheeled sulkies, fifty pounds heavier than those used today.) She lowered her own mark six more times, and at 21 turned in a mile that was only two seconds off her own world's record. Her fame was such that whole villages used to come down to the depot for a glimpse of her when she passed through in her private car. In the fall of 1876 all the employees of a large shoe factory in North Brookfield, Mass., walked out for the day to see her perform at Springfield, 35 miles away. In thirteen years of competition she didn't miss a single performance. There was never a trotter like the Goldsmith Maid.

The Hambletonian, held annually on various tracks since 1926, is the Kentucky Derby of harness horse racing. It is the oldest trotting race in the land, offers a rich purse and carries the most prestige. It was named in honor of the great sire Rysdyk's Hambletonian, shown here in his stall with owner Rysdyk himself. Strangely, the horse was not much of a trotter. Rysdyk, a canny Dutch-American farm hand, was aware of the horse's potentialities as a sire and was loathe to let him appear on the track. The few times he did appear, mostly in exhibition heats, Rysdyk himself drove him. The policy paid off handsomely. As Hambletonian's fame grew, his stud fee increased. From $25 it went to $35, then to $75, $100, $300, and, for the last ten years of his career at stud, $500. Rysdyk, who had paid a farmer $125 for the stallion, realized more than $200,000 on his investment. The high fees were not out of line, for many of Hambletonian's 1,331 foals became famous trotters, and they in turn sired many others. His offspring were noted for their speed and stamina. The great stallion, who died in 1876, contributed more to the development of the standard breed than any other horse.

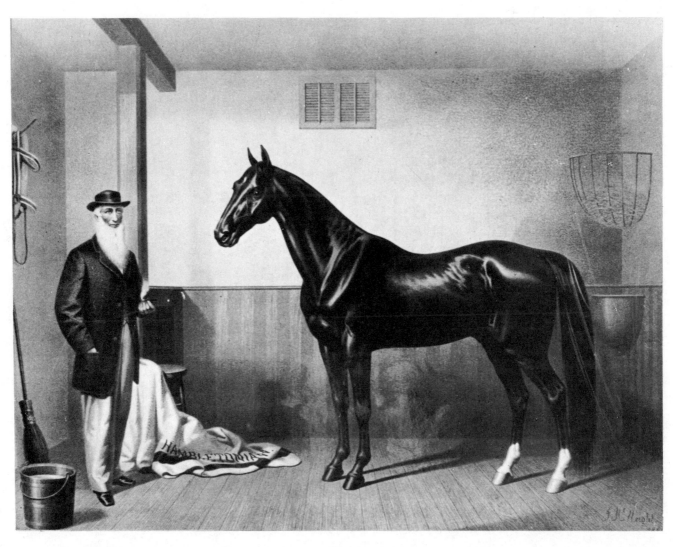

One of the first six-oared shells in the country (below) was built for Harvard in 1857 at St. Johns, New Brunswick. Far lighter than the barges then in use, it enabled the Harvards to win all their races, until the design was copied by other colleges.

Rowing became a big intercollegiate sport in the 1870's. Below left, the Yale crew returns from a practice spin on Lake Saratoga, New York, 1874. Cartoon below shows a muscular, low-browed oarsman winning the girl while the campus intellectual chokes with frustration.

THE VICTORY OF MUSCLE OVER MIND.

Lake Saratoga was the site of a great intercollegiate regatta on July 14, 1875 (above) when thirteen six-man crews rowed a three-mile course. The field included the entire Ivy League (less Penn) plus Wesleyan, Amherst, Williams, Bowdoin, Hamilton and Union. Cornell led the field, finishing in 16 minutes, 53¼ seconds. The regatta was such an unwieldy affair that Yale and Harvard withdrew from the Rowing Association and from 1876 on staged their own regattas.

November 6, 1869, was a memorable day in football history, for on that day the first intercollegiate game was played when Rutgers and Princeton clashed at New Brunswick, New Jersey. This picture, which now hangs in the Football Hall of Fame at Rutgers, was painted in 1932 by W. M. Boyd. The artist interviewed the few old players who were then alive, and the painting is an accurate representation of the first game. Under the rules agreed upon, there were twenty-five men on a side. It was a running, kicking, continuous game, but the players could not run with the round rubber ball. They could catch it, however, for a free kick and bat it with their hands to advance it. It was soccer with minor changes. To distinguish themselves from the Princetons, the Rutgers players wore scarlet caps or flaming red jerseys. It was agreed that the team which first

scored six goals would be the winner. A goal was one point, earned by kicking the ball under the crossbars. Rutgers won, 6 to 4, and thus became the first college football team in history to defeat another college. (In England football was not taken up by the colleges until 1872; it was played only in secondary schools prior to that date.) A second game was played in Princeton a week later which the Tigers won, 8 to 0, but the rubber match was not held. The next year Rutgers beat Columbia, 6 to 3, in the only game played, and there were no more played until 1872, when Yale and Columbia met. So far there was no uniformity of rules, and the game was a mongrel type of football, neither soccer, rugby, nor American football. But before long it was to develop into a distinctly American game, which would become our number-one intercollegiate sport.

No one invented American football. Like baseball, it developed from English sources, but one man more than anyone else caused its transformation into the modern game. He is Walter Camp (above), "The Father of American Football." He was the great architect of the game. He played football at Yale for six years, was captain for three years and a member of the Intercollegiate Football Rules Committee for forty-eight years. In 1891 he wrote the first book ever published on the game. Camp had a penetrative mind and introduced rules which changed the game from rugby to American football. He created the scrimmage line, the eleven-man team, signal calling, and the quarterback position. Most important, he originated the rule whereby a team had to give up the ball unless it was advanced five yards in three consecutive downs (now ten yards, four downs). This is the heart of today's game. Camp also introduced a rule which permitted tackling below the waist.

(The picture above shows the high tackle in vogue before 1888.) Camp was for years football's one-man authority. He collaborated with Casper Whitney, editor of *The Week's Sport*, in picking the first All-America teams and was the recognized arbiter of the selections until his death in 1925. Football would not be what it is today without Camp's influence.

The influence of the "scrum" in rugby is evident in this old photograph, showing how the ball was put into play in the game's early days. The center did not pass the ball between his legs but kicked it to the quarterback directly behind him, who ran with it while the rest of the team gave him what interference it could. His teammates would grab him and push, pull, or yank him along in any direction in an attempt to advance the ball. Meanwhile opposing tacklers would be clinging to him, trying to hold him back. The result was that often there would be twenty-one men clustered around the ball carrier, all pushing and pulling him in opposite directions. It's a wonder he didn't get torn apart.

Unwieldy as the game was by modern standards, sizeable crowds turned out to see the Harvard, Yale, and Princeton contests. At the left is a woodcut of the Yale-Princeton game which was played in the rain on Thanksgiving Day, 1886. A scoreless tie was the result.

Before 1888, when all tackling was above the waist, a runner could employ the straight arm with great effect, much more so than today. The picture on the right shows how difficult it was for a tackler to bring his man down when he couldn't dive for the legs. The straight arm was one of the first fundamentals taught to a backfield man in the early days of the game.

Below is a cartoon of a Yale-Princeton game which the artist satirically titled, "Cheerful sport between the aesthetic young gentlemen of Princeton and Yale." The game wasn't quite as violent as this exaggerated cartoon indicates, but it was rough enough, so much so that the captains of five Ivy League colleges got together in 1889 in attempt to discourage slugging and swearing.

For a quarter of a century after the Civil War, football was largely confined to the big Eastern colleges, with Harvard, Yale, Princeton (The Big Three), and Penn dominating the game. On the first ten All-America teams (1889–1898), only two players were selected who did not come from one of these four universities. They were Wycoff of Cornell, 1895, and Herschberger of Chicago, 1898. Several smaller colleges in the East took up the game, but they were no match for the Big Three. These matches were considered practice games, mere tune-ups for the real games at the season's end. An example is the Yale-Wesleyan series in 1886, when the teams met three times. Yale won the first two, 75–0 and 62–0, and Wesleyan, encouraged by its improved showing in the second game, asked for another try. They dropped this one, 136–0. Even so, Wesleyan was good enough to beat Lafayette 26–0 that year, which demonstrates the vast difference in the caliber of play in those days between the Ivy League giants and the other colleges. It was not to be so for very long. The game rapidly spread throughout the East, went west of the Alleghenies in the '80's, and by 1892 was established on the West Coast, when Stanford and California met. Before the turn of the century, football conferences had come into existence, natural rivalries had sprung up, and the game was being played in every section of the country by colleges, prep schools, and high schools. The East still turned out the best teams, but it no longer owned the game.

The pictures on this page show the standard uniform of the '90's and the blunt-nosed ball then in use. The laced canvas jacket, devised to prevent a tackler from getting a handhold on a man, was first worn in 1877. Tight canvas pants were also used at first, but they were replaced in 1888 by moleskin pants, which gave better protection against leg bruises and were more comfortable. Headguards were unknown, and players used to let their hair grow long to absorb shock.

The annual Thanksgiving Day game between Yale and Princeton, held in New York in the '90's, was the most glamorous sporting event in the country. The collegians, wearing huge greatcoats and ulsters and carrying banners and canes wrapped in ribbons, formed a steady procession up Fifth Avenue on the morning of the game, riding in everything on four wheels that could hold them. It was the outdoor social event of the season, a spectacle that old timers still remember with pleasure.

At that time, mass plays, such as the one shown below, characterized the game, and deception played little part. The flying wedge, the turtle back, the tackle tandem were all variations of the mass attack in which the ball carrier was hidden within a human fortress. Weight and momentum were all-important as the fearsome thing rolled forward like a tank. Serious injuries often resulted when two teams met head on from a flying start.

The game really belonged to the boys in the gas-lit era; the coach was merely an advisor. The captain was the head man. He picked the team, ran it with complete authority, and, in most colleges, had the power to fire the coach. It was a bruising, bone-breaking game in those days, and players trained like prize fighters. They scrimmaged for hours every day, took long hikes on Sundays, and played regular games twice a week. The games consisted of two 45-minute halves, and, unless there was an injury, the eleven men who started a game finished it. Substitutions were not allowed until the late '80's, and then only for injuries. When a player was removed from the field he was through for the day. It was considered more or less of a disgrace to be taken out of a game for any reason short of unconsciousness.

The mop-headed old timers may seem quaint and slightly ridiculous in the light of today, but they weren't. They were rugged and they loved the game. And it belonged to them.

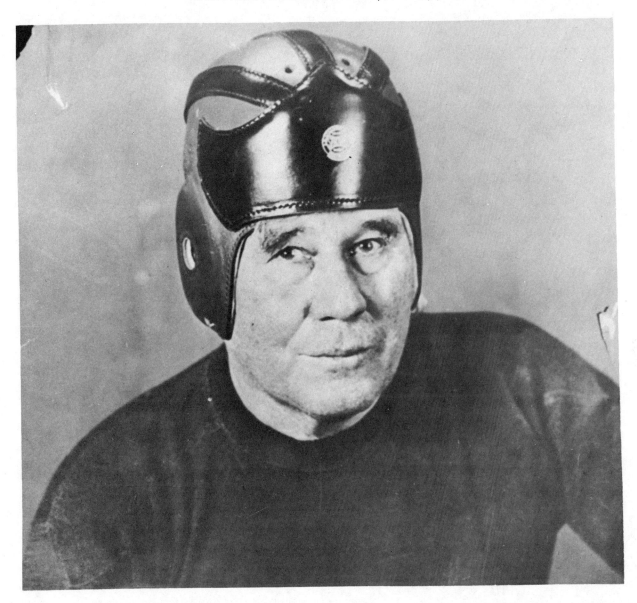

Walter W. (Pudge) Heffelfinger, shown here as he was about to play his last game at the age of 65, knew the old game as well as the modern one. (He'll take the old one.) Pudge is the Paul Bunyan of football, the game's living legend, and the only player to be chosen on *every* All-Time All-Player list since the first one was compiled in 1904. Grantland Rice selected him on his Eternal All-America in 1939, and in 1951 he was named on the first team for the Rutgers Football Hall of Fame. Pudge played guard at Yale from 1888 to 1890 and continued to play until 1933. He has been called the most devastating player ever seen on a football field. Fast, powerful, and alert, he stood six feet, two inches, and weighed 200 pounds. He was the first lineman to pull himself out of the line and run interference for the backs, a feat which he performed with amazing effect. In 1922, when he was 53, he captained a team in a charity game in Columbus (he never played pro ball) and was the outstanding man on the field. No other player was over 30. Bo McMillin, his teammate, said after the game, "He was absolutely unbelievable. I never saw anything like him." Grantland Rice, who was there, said that Pudge at the age of 53 was still the best guard in the country. In view of his long career on the gridiron (45 years) and the fact that he has made every All-Star, All-Time team, it is probable that Heffelfinger was the greatest lineman who ever lived.

In 1873, at a Christmas party in Wales, Major Walter C. Wingfield (left) introduced a game which he called "Sphairistike, or Lawn Tennis." With him he had a set of printed rules and the implements of play. The Major's game, an outdoor adaptation of the ancient game of court tennis (above), was played on an hour-glass-shaped court, with a box in the center of one court for the service area. Outdoor tennis had been played in England before the Major introduced his game and rule book. Nevertheless, he took out a patent on Sphairistike, claiming that he was the inventor of the game. Whether he was or not, the awkward Greek name, meaning "ball-play," was soon dropped, and the game officially became lawn tennis when the Marylebone Cricket Club issued its tennis rules in 1875. This was the real beginning of lawn tennis, which today is the most popular court game ever devised.

A year after Major Wingfield uncorked his game in Wales, a fellow army officer took some equipment to Bermuda, where he was stationed, and introduced the game there. Among the vacationists was Miss Mary E. Outerbridge of Staten Island, who tried the new sport and liked it well enough to bring a set home with her. She had some trouble getting the net, racket, and balls through the customs because the officials had never seen anything like them before. Finally she got the stuff through, and a week later the first court in this country was laid out at the Staten Island Cricket and Baseball Club. This was in the Spring of 1874, less than a year after the Major first pronounced "Sphairistike!" The game was at first considered a girlish pastime by the young men of Staten Island, but they soon saw that it required agility and accuracy and they began to take it up. In a short time courts were laid out in Lakewood, New Jersey, Tuxedo Park, New York, and Newport, Rhode Island. No other game has ever spread so rapidly in such a short time.

The first important tournament (below) was held at Staten Island in 1880, by which time more than thirty clubs in the East had tennis courts. Not until the following year, however, when the U.S. Lawn Tennis Association was formed, was a tournament held under uniform rules, open to all comers. This marked the beginning of the U.S.L.T.A.-sanctioned championships, which have been held every year since 1881.

The first winner was Richard D. (Dicky) Sears (left), who kept right on winning for seven consecutive years.

The sport in Dicky's time was confined to a few wealthy people in the East and was considered a sissy game by nonplayers. This cartoon (right) shows how they felt about it. The sight of two grown men patting a ball back and forth across a net and shouting "Love!" at each other was a little too much for the man in the street to stand.

Drawing below of a photo taken in 1899 of the Staten Island courts points out the change in dress in nineteen years as well as the increasing popularity of the game.

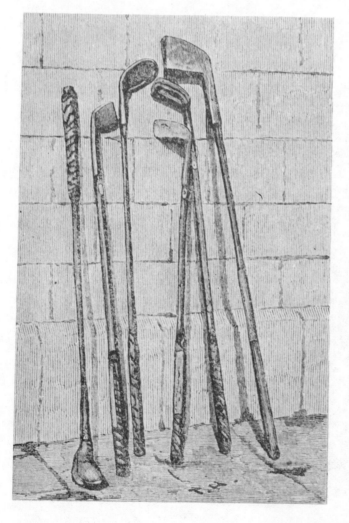

This is the first photograph ever taken of a golf match played on American soil. It was taken in 1888 and shows the first green of the original St. Andrews course at Yonkers, New York. The land on which the six-hole course was laid out belonged to John Shotts, a local butcher, who permitted the golfing pioneers to knock their gutta-percha balls around his thirty-acre lot rent free. Golf had been played here before 1888, but St. Andrews was the first permanent golf club established in this country. It has been in continuous existence since November 14, 1888, when John Reid, a transplanted Scot, formed the club at a dinner party for four golfing cronies at his Yonkers home. Reid, "the Father of American Golf," stands on the extreme right in the above picture. Robert Lockhart, another Scot, should also be given credit for starting the game here. Like Reid, Lockhart was born in Dunfermline, Scotland, and lived in Yonkers. In 1887, on a visit to Dunfermline, Lockhart purchased a set of golf clubs and two dozen guttie balls and brought them back to Yonkers.

The original golf sticks consisted of a driver, brassie, spoon, cleek, sand iron, and putter. They were carried loose over the shoulder, like fagots, in the pre-golf-bag days. One extra ball was all a player needed since few were lost.

Moving a clubhouse and laying out a new course was an easy matter for the St. Andrews golfers. When they decided to move, in 1892, they picked up the tent that had served as a clubhouse, carried it a quarter of a mile up the road to an apple orchard, and in one day laid out a six-hole course. Two years later they moved again, this time into an old farmhouse at Grey Oaks, which they transformed into a real clubhouse. Here the club came into full flower. A nine-hole course was laid out—this one took two days—and the members adopted a uniform of scarlet coats with brass buttons, gray knickers, plaid hose, and gray gaiters. The winged collar and cap was *de rigueur* on the course.

When the St. Andrews golfers moved, in 1897, to their present home at Mount Hope, they left behind at Grey Oaks this old well (left), which is revered as the original nineteenth hole. Water only.

The Old
Well
of Genl Odell

A Welcome and a
Cool Drink

By 1893 the game had spread to Chicago, where the nation's first eighteen-hole course was built. The Chicago Golf Club's top man was Charles B. Macdonald (above), who came East to Newport in 1895 to win the first amateur championship conducted by the newly formed U.S. Golf Association. (The year before, Macdonald was runner-up in two amateur championship tournaments at Newport and St. Andrews, but these were held before the U.S.G.A. was formed.) Macdonald, then, was the first official amateur golf champion of the United States, a title he never won again, although he tried many times. In 1910 Macdonald designed and built the National Golf Links at Southampton, Long Island, America's first course of championship caliber.

Three years after the founding of St. Andrews, the United States had for the first time a golf course that could really be called a golf course. This was Shinnecock Hills at Southampton, which was built by Willie Dunn, a Scotch professional. Dunn came to this country in March, 1891, and, with a crew of 150 Indians from the Shinnecock reservation, cleared 4,000 acres of thick brush and laid out a twelve-hole seaside links. By June the job was finished. The new game was so popular among the Southamptonites that they decided to incorporate and build a clubhouse. Stanford White, the foremost architect in the country, designed it. The stock, offered at $100 per share, was immediately oversubscribed. In the summer of 1892 the club, with a membership of seventy, was formally opened. Thus, Shinnecock Hills became the first golf club on Long Island, the first in the United States to be incorporated and have a clubhouse, and the first to have a waiting list.

Charlie Macdonald, the golfer in the center in the picture below, deserves a niche in golf's Hall of Fame for being the first to introduce the alibi to American golf. When he was beaten by one stroke at Newport in 1894 in the first amateur (though unofficial) championship, he claimed that the two-stroke penalty imposed when he removed his ball from a stone wall was not a legitimate penalty. Furthermore, said Charlie, medal play was no way to conduct an amateur championship, and he refused to recognize his conqueror, W. G. Lawrence. A month later, at match play at St. Andrews in the second amateur championship held that year, Macdonald again went down to defeat, this time at the hands of Lawrence B. Stoddard. Once more Charlie came up with an alibi. He hadn't felt well at lunch before his final match, he said, and on the advice of a friend he had consumed a big steak and a bottle of champagne. It was the lunch, Charlie claimed, that caused him to slice his drive into a ploughed field and lose the match on the nineteenth hole. The picture below was taken during one of the early rounds of the St. Andrews tournament and shows (from left to right) James Park, of the Richmond Country Club, Laurence Curtis, of The Country Club, Macdonald, George Armstrong of St. Andrews, and Louis Biddle, of the Philadelphia Country Club.

John L. Sullivan was the most popular fighter who ever lived. He was America's first great sports hero, the first to be followed on the streets by admiring throngs. He looked this way in the early 1880's at the beginning of his career—trim, fit, and ready to stand up against any man in the world.

He fought with bare fists, with skin-tight or padded gloves, under the London Prize Ring or Marquis of Queensberry Rules—anyway at all. For ten years (1882–1892) he ruled the roost, supreme and unbeatable. They called him the Boston Strong Boy, but he was more than merely strong. He was amazingly fast for a big man and had a knock-em-dead punch in either hand. Ring science was not for John L. He never bothered much with defense. He brushed aside blows and kept moving forward, always punching. His was a hurricane attack.

The sporting world first heard about the young giant (5 feet, 10½ inches, 200 pounds in condition) when he flattened a series of opponents in various Boston theaters. The bouts were billed as exhibitions, and the glove-wearing boxers were supposed to take it easy, but John L. didn't know what sparring meant. The first time he ever fought—it was against an experienced pug named Scannell, who challenged anyone in the theater to stay three rounds—John L. hit him so hard that Scannell sailed out of the ring over the footlights and landed in the orchestra pit. Young

Sullivan's fame quickly spread as he whipped such ring notables as the Western champion, John Donaldson, Joe Goss, ex-champion of England and America, and Jack Stewart, the Canadian title holder.

His first real test came in 1881, when the 22-year-old fighter came to New York to meet John Flood, the Bull's Head Terror. Flood was a waterfront tough, leader of the city's most infamous gang, and had never been beaten. Sullivan and Flood met at night on a barge tied up to a Yonkers dock and fought under the dim flare of gas lamps. The picture below shows what happened after sixteen minutes of fighting, when the battered Flood went down for the last time. In the crowd was Paddy Ryan, the champion. After John L. had lifted the senseless Flood off the deck and delivered him to his seconds, he turned to Ryan and grinned, "Ready for yours, Paddy?" Paddy was ready a year later and went the same way Flood did in a nine-round bare-knuckle fight. "When Sullivan hit me," said Ryan afterwards, "I thought a telegraph pole had been shoved against me endways." John L. could hit.

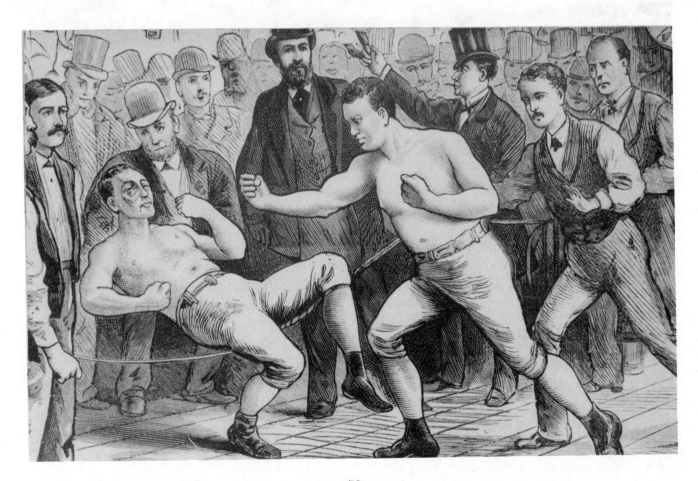

79

For the next ten years Sullivan was generally accepted as the world's champion, but there were two fighters who stuck in his craw. One was Charley Mitchell, claimant to the English throne, who survived a thirty-nine-round, three-hour bare-fist fight by running away, until the bout was halted by a heavy rainstorm. John L. was not once off his feet; Mitchell went down thirty-nine times. Nevertheless, the fight was declared a draw. The other was Jake Kilrain of Baltimore, named champion by Richard K. Fox, publisher of the *Police Gazette*. Fox had no right to do this, but he hated Sullivan and wanted his own man on the throne. Fox's sporting weekly flung constant challenges at the real champion, and at last Sullivan answered (left) with a challenge of his own. Fox, as Kilrain's backer, covered the $10,000 bet, and the two champions met at Richburg, Mississippi, on July 8, 1889, in what was to be the last championship bare-knuckle fight of all time.

Glove bouts and the Queensberry rules had made their appearance a few years before, but the "pillows" were still looked upon with scorn by most fight fans, as the cartoon below indicates. The Sullivan-Kilrain mill was going to be no fancy sparring match, it was going to be a real old-fashioned bare-fist fight to a finish.

About 3,000 rabid fans were present on that broiling July morning (106° in the shade) when the two men were called to scratch, shortly after ten o'clock. The question was, could Sullivan last in a long battle. He'd been living riotously for years, drunk more often than sober, and he was now thirty years old. Kilrain, a good wrestler and a fair puncher, had been trained by Charley Mitchell for a marathon of fighting. He was in shape to go all day. If he could get by Sullivan's first furious assaults, he could come on to win, Mitchell thought. So did the fans, although they favored John L. slightly in the betting. They liked what they saw when the Big Fellow discarded his bathrobe and stood resplendent in green knee breeches, flesh-colored stockings, and black boots laced high over the ankles. Except for a slight roll around his middle, he looked fit.

Kilrain followed his battle plan to the letter by keeping away from the always advancing Sullivan, refusing to swap punches, and clinching frequently to gain a fall. The rare photo on the opposite page shows the two fighters in a clinch in the seventh round—the only bare-knuckle bout ever photographed. It was Sullivan who was supposed to tire first as the fight wore on, but instead he grew stronger. He didn't even sit down once between rounds. "What the hell's the use?" he told his anxious handlers. "I got to get right up again, ain't I?" Sullivan scored all the knockdowns, Kilrain most of the falls, but it was John L. who did the damage. Gradually Kilrain weakened to the point where his blows had no force at all. But he kept on, staggering to scratch with blood running from his ears and nose. Then he'd back-pedal to avoid punishment. "Why don't you stand up and fight? You're supposed to be the champ, ain't you?" taunted Sullivan as he pursued his man. During the seventy-fifth round a physician said to Mike Donovan, Kilrain's second, "If you keep sending him out there, he'll die." Donovan, who had seen two men killed in the ring, threw in the sponge, and the fight was over. It had taken 2 hours and 16 minutes to prove that John L. was the real champion.

GLOVES.

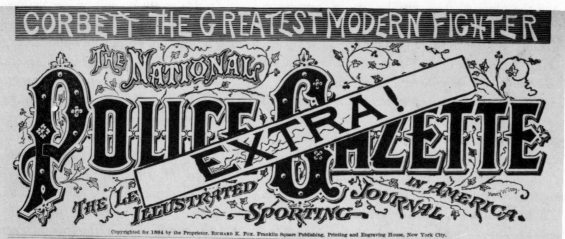

CORBETT'S VICTORY CREATES WILD ENTHUSIASM.
THE CONQUEROR OF MITCHELL GIVEN AN OVATION IN THE CLUB ARENA IN JACKSONVILLE, FLA.
DRAWN BY "POLICE GAZETTE" SPECIAL ARTISTS.

"Corbett the Greatest Modern Fighter" said the *Police Gazette* on the cover of its issue of February 10, 1894, and there are many old-timers around today who will tell you that the words are still true—old-timers who have seen all the heavyweights since Corbett. James J. Corbett was a San Francisco bank clerk, a clean-living, well-conditioned athlete, who stood an inch over six feet and fought at 184 pounds. He was the antithesis of the roaring John L. in every way. He was well mannered, brainy, modest, and as nimble footed as a figure skater. He couldn't hit like Sullivan, but he could do things Sullivan never dreamed of. He could feint, slip punches, side-step, and counter with a left jab so fast that it was a blur to the eye. Sullivan had nothing but contempt for this "fancy dude," as he called Corbett, but agreed to take him on in a glove fight in New Orleans on September 7, 1892. Sullivan was twenty pounds overweight and had not fought in three years, but what did it matter? He'd been invincible for a decade and still carried a mule's kick in either hand. He was a one-to-four favorite, and no one thought Corbett had a chance—no one except Corbett, who said, "I can lick him without getting my hair mussed." His boast described the fight. It was pitiful. Sullivan was unable to land one solid punch, and in the twenty-first round he sank to the floor, more from exhaustion than anything else, and was counted out for the first time in his life.

This was the first championship fight in which padded gloves were used, the first under the Queensberry rules, and it marked a turning point in ring history. Gone forever were the old mauling sluggers, to be replaced by a new school of faster, more scientific boxers. The marathon had given way to the sprint.

Next on Corbett's list was Charley Mitchell, the little Englishman (158 pounds) who had been such a thorn in John L.'s side. It took only three rounds for Corbett to flatten him and thus to become undisputed champion of the world. The *Gazette* cover (opposite page) shows handsome Jim being carried from the ring in triumph.

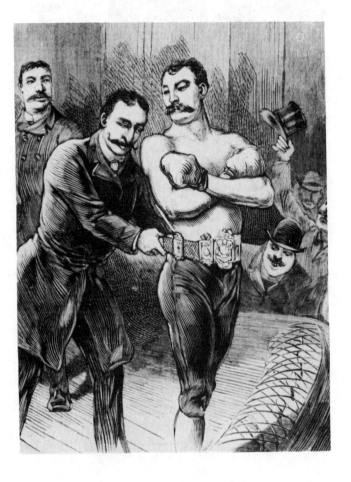

Richard K. Fox, shown above awarding the *Police Gazette* belt to Jake Kilrain, was as strong for Corbett as he had been against John L. Now that the young Californian had conquered Sullivan and Mitchell there was no questioning his right to the championship of the world. By whipping the American and British champions he became the undisputed title-holder, the first American to gain recognition on both sides of the Atlantic.

Fox gave away more than a quarter of a million dollars in cash prizes, medals, belts, and trophies to boost circulation and promote himself. He was a genius at beating the tom-toms for the glory of the *Gazette* and for Fox.

On these two pages are shown some of the many and weird Fox-sponsored events. Above, left, is George A. Sampson, a champion strong man (Fox used the word "champion" to describe almost anything that moved, as long as it moved for the *Gazette*), in the act of supporting a scale-model Ferris wheel on his chest. The year before (1893), the first passenger-carrying Ferris wheel was in operation at the World's Fair in Chicago. Also on display there was Sandow, a strong man who was exhibited by young Flo Ziegfeld. But Fox strove to outdo both the Chicago Ferris wheel and Sandow

by having the *Police Gazette* strong man lift the *Police Gazette* Ferris wheel for a prize.

In the same way he had his own man, Lawrence M. Donovan, take a plunge off the Brooklyn Bridge (above, right) to make people forget about Steve Brodie, who pioneered the act in 1886 to gain national fame of a sort.

Fox loved seeing his own face in his weekly and on the various cups and medals he passed out so freely. On the opposite page, above, is a typical Fox award, showing the publisher's moustachioed features in the center of the bauble won by Billy Wells for allowing his cranium to be sledge-hammered through a block of iron.

Below it is a more prosaic *Gazette*-sponsored event, a single-sculls race, which was won by one Albert Hamm.

84

Fox's story is like that of the Horatio Alger heroes who flourished during his time. An immigrant from Dublin, the 29-year-old Fox arrived here in 1874, without friends and with only a few shillings in his pocket. He got a job on a New York newspaper, and in two years had saved a couple of hundred dollars, which, added to a few hundred more which he borrowed, was enough to purchase the *Gazette*. It was the oldest weekly in the country, but its circulation had dried up when Fox took over. One of the first things he did was to start a sports section, a feature unknown in the daily newspapers then. Fox knew little about sports, but he had a hunch that people were interested in them, particularly in prize fighting, which was illegal, but fascinating to many. In 1880, when a match was made between England's Joe Goss and Paddy Ryan of Troy, New York, for the American title, Fox assigned several artists and reporters to give the fight full coverage. After the battle (won by Ryan in 87 rounds), the *Gazette* launched a special edition, which had the only full account of the fray, plus ringside pictures. The result was astounding. For weeks the *Gazette* presses kept rolling to fill the demand. Circulation zoomed to new heights. Fox, the poor immigrant lad, made millions on his hunch that America wanted to read about sports.

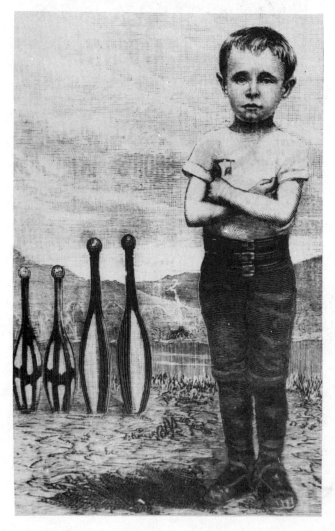

The astonishing success of the new *Gazette* made newspaper editors aware of the circulation value of more sports coverage. At first they assigned general reporters to cover sporting events, but, as they became specialists in their field, editors tended to use them for sports exclusively. Soon separate sports sections began to appear in the larger dailies. It was Fox, then, who more or less forced the sports pages into existence.

Fox played his hunch to the limit, promoting every kind of sports event and awarding sports much space in the *Gazette's* pink pages. Many of the tournaments he sponsored had nothing to do with athletic prowess. For example, he once offered a gold belt to the bartender who could make a *pousse café* with the most layers. The winner created one with fourteen layers, each a different color. He ran a hair-cutting contest against time with clippers barred and only regulation scissors permitted. The winning barber turned in a performance of less than thirty seconds. He gave prizes for competitive oyster-opening, steeple-climbing, singing, rowing, shooting, and one-legged dancing.

Fox recognized champions in the animal world, such as the best rat-catcher and the outstanding fighting dog, the latter shown here (above, left) with his owner, Tim McGraw.

Below McGraw stands little Johnny Wessles, the *Gazette's* champion club-swinger, boy's division. And on the opposite page are two lady pugilists having a go for a *Gazette* laurel. (Fox never took female fighting seriously, but he did crown the woman champion of New York, a powerful Amazon named Alice Jennings, who had a great left hook.)

Quaint and corny as many of these gag tournaments may seem to us today, it must be remembered that in Fox's day there were few sports as we now know them. And most of them, such as the ring, the cock pit, and the fighting-dog arena, were on the illegal side. Baseball, for example, didn't really get started until the National League was founded in 1876, the year Fox bought the *Gazette*.

Fox's pink pages may seem hilarious today, but he was doing no more than reflecting the times, giving fans the sports they wanted to read about. And almost every male in the United States read the *Gazette*—even Jesse James, who dropped Fox a note from Sempronius, Texas, saying, "Have been on the move so much lately that I have not received the *Police Gazette* regularly. Please send copy here and oblige, Jesse James." The paper was indeed the sporting man's Bible, and Fox, while still in his mid-thirties, became the most influential figure in the sport's world, the final arbiter in all things athletic. He looked the part, too. A natty dresser, slim and autocratic, he epitomized the sporting man of the gas-lit era. But, more important, he was the first to realize that America had become sports-conscious.

The Cincinnati Red Stockings, baseball's first professional team, brought so much glory to the Rhineland City in the first two years of its existence (1869–1870) that most of the other leading amateurs decided to turn pro, too. The amateur game began to fade into the background when ten club delegates met in New York in March, 1871, to establish the National Association of Professional Base-Ball Players. The first professional league was loosely bound, with no fixed schedule and no control over its members. In many parks, bookmakers ran booths openly where fans and players could put down bets on or against themselves. As professional gamblers took over, attendance fell off everywhere, clubs lost money, and the game almost passed into oblivion. It was saved by the efforts of William A. Hulbert, owner of the Chicago club, and Albert G. Spalding, star pitcher for the Bostons. Hulbert conferred with Spalding and called a meeting of the eight league members to take place in New York on February 2, 1876. Hulbert persuaded the magnates to abolish gambling, liquor selling on club grounds, and the buying of pool tickets by players. He produced a model constitution for a more efficiently operated league, which he called the National League of Professional Base Ball Clubs. All the eight magnates signed, and thus the National League came into existence.

The game's greatest pitcher in the 1870's was Albert G. Spalding, who is remembered today more for the sporting-goods house which he founded than for his twirling ability. Using the underhand delivery, he pitched the Bostons to four straight pennants (1872–1875) and was on the mound in almost every game. In 1874, for example, Boston won 52 games and lost 18; so did Spalding, who pitched every game that season. Spalding was a right-hander, stood six feet, two inches, and threw a fast ball with a change of pace. Hulbert persuaded him to jump to the Chicago White Stockings, and when the news leaked out, while the pitcher was still with Boston, kids used to follow him on the streets and shout, "Oh, you seceder. Your White Stockings will get dirty."

Cap Anson was another star brought to Chicago by Hulbert in 1876. An Iowa farm boy, he was christened Adrian Constantine Anson, but he was Cap to everyone, and the nickname is on his plaque in Baseball's Hall of Fame today. Cap was the outstanding player of the last century and the most durable one the game has ever known. He played major-league ball for twenty-seven years, and only twice did he hit under .300. Twice he was over the .400 mark. In 1897, his last year, he batted .302 at the age of forty-six. Cap's regular position was first base, but he could play any infield position well and often caught. As manager of Chicago for nineteen years, he led the team to five championships.

5 1/4 OZ

PECK & SNYDER'S

PROFFESSIONAL DEAD BALL
1 OUNCE VULCANIZED RUBBER

9 1/4 INCH

The White Stockings of the '80's were the Yankees of their time; Cap Anson's brawny lads—they were all six-footers—completely dominated the National League. The Chicago fans idolized them and dubbed them the "Heroic Legion of Baseball." One season, on a trip to Washington, the team was received by President Grover Cleveland at the White House (above). The men lined up, and each took a turn at shaking the President's hand. Mike (King) Kelly, the slugging catcher, later wrote of the interview, "The President's hand was fat and soft. I squeezed it so hard that he winced." Kelly said that every member of the team gave the President a powerhouse grip. "His right hand was almost double in size and he was glad when it was all over. He didn't shake hands with us again when we parted," Kelly observed. Stalwart lads were the old White Stockings.

At the close of the 1888 season, the White Stockings and a picked National League team started west on an around-the-world tour. They gave exhibitions in Hawaii, New Zealand, Australia, Egypt, and several European countries. In England, they received this polite but rather stuffy note (right) from the Prince of Wales, stating that he found baseball interesting but considered cricket superior.

The Britishers were puzzled by baseball and looked upon it as a glorified game of rounders. The cartoon below, from an English humorous weekly, pokes fun at the American game. The English kid says to the gigantic overstuffed catcher, "Look 'ere, Mister, we represents the 'Ackney Boys Rounders Club, and we're game to play you any Sat'day you likes and give you fust innings."

Ned Hanlon, shown here at ease in a photographer's studio, was the game's first strategist, the originator of inside baseball. A player of only ordinary ability himself, Hanlon rose to fame as manager of the Baltimore Orioles (1892–1898), where he developed such Hall-of-Famers as John McGraw, Willie Keeler, Wilbert Robinson, and Hughey Jennings. Hanlon's boys were aggressive, colorful, and imaginative. They were the first to employ the bunt, the hit-and-run play, the squeeze, and the double steal. They were so baffling that John Ward, manager of the Giants, once threatened to bring Hanlon before league headquarters. Ward said that the Orioles were not playing baseball but a new game outside the rules.

One of Hanlon's prize pupils was Wee Willie Keeler, a five-foot, four-inch mite, who was the greatest place hitter of all time. The Wee one was no slugger, and the outfielders knew it. They used to play in so close that there would be seven men in the infield trying to stop him. Willie didn't mind, he drove the ball right through them. The secret of his uncanny stick work, as he explained to a sports writer, was "I hit 'em where they ain't." Using the short grip on the bat, Willie averaged .393 in his five years with the Orioles. One year he stole 73 bases. He was an all-around man, a left-hander who normally played the outfield but could perform as a shortstop or third baseman as well.

Hurling himself at the plate in a desperate slide is Buck Ewing, the peerless Giant backstop. Actually, Buck had to hold this pose for a time exposure of several seconds in Goodwin's studio in New York, where many ball players of the '80's had their pictures taken. On the field Buck was not as laughable as he looks in this picture. He had a great arm, and there were few runners who dared to steal on him. He was a better than .300 hitter and a clever base runner. Buck was the first of the modern school of catchers, and some say he was the greatest.

Cy Young (right), the most durable pitcher of them all, is the only man to win more than 500 games, a record that will undoubtedly stand forever. In his twenty-two-year career (1890–1911) in both major leagues, he won a total of 511. Walter Johnson, with 414 victories, is the only hurler to break 400, so Cy's mark seems safe. Young had all the assets required of a super pitcher—speed, control, a curve, coolness under fire, and an iron arm. He had it all. Cy had three no-hitters in his record book, and one of them was a perfect game in which no opposing batsman reached first base.

Dr. James Naismith, shown here as he looked in 1933, is the inventor of the only sport purely American in origin. Basketball, unlike baseball, football, and golf, is one of the few sports that is not the result of a long evolutionary process. It was the brain child of one man, who was, incidentally, born in Canada. Naismith attended McGill University, at Montreal, and later taught physical education at the Y.M.C.A. Training College at Springfield, Mass. (now called Springfield College). At the end of the football season in 1891, Dr. Naismith put his mind to work devising an indoor recreation which would appeal to the football players, who were reluctant to face a winter of calisthenics and gymnastics. Some kind of a team game would be the thing, thought the doctor. A soccer ball would do as a starter, and the goal should be out of reach so that men playing in scanty gym suits on hard floors wouldn't get hurt in mix-ups at the mouth of the goal. Skill rather than force should be stressed, he reasoned. After some experimenting, Dr. Naismith had a couple of old peach baskets fastened to the railing of the gym balcony and directed the boys to shoot at them with the soccer ball.

The drawing on the right, showing the first basketball game ever played, is in the possession of Springfield College, where experimental games were first tried in the winter of 1891. The game was officially born in January, 1892, when Dr. Naismith printed the first set of regulations under the heading "A New Game." Note the man on the ladder standing by to remove the ball from the peach basket and toss it back into play.

At first teams consisted of nine men, then seven, and finally five. Below is the first basketball team, consisting of nine players, and their coach, Dr. Naismith, on the steps of the Springfield College gymnasium in 1891. As the game progressed it occurred to someone that if the bottom of the peach basket were removed the ball would drop through it and then there would be no need for the man on the ladder.

Track and field games in the gas-lit era, as evidenced in these two pictures, were crude affairs by today's standards. The hurdles stretched all the way across the track, and, when a man knocked one down, it was down for all. Runners used the standing start even after C. H. Sherrill, a Yale sprinter of the late '80's, introduced the crouching start and ran away from everybody. (Below is the start of the hundred-yard dash at the intercollegiate games in 1890.) The New York Athletic Club was the pioneer in amateur track and field in this country. In 1871, three years after the N.Y.A.C. was founded, the club built the first cinder track in America and invited track athletes from all over to compete at its annual games. The sport spread to the colleges, and in 1874 the first intercollegiate track meet was held at Saratoga in conjunction with the regatta.

American athletes in the first modern Olympic Games, held at Athens in 1896, ran away with so many track and field events that they were charged with being professionals. In truth, they were the purest of the pure—a handful of college athletes who paid their own way to make the trip and were not even champions in their own country. In the twelve-event track and field program, the Americans put men in every event except the 800-meter run and scored nine wins in eleven tries. The Greeks got one victory, but it was the one they wanted most—the marathon. (Above, Spiridon Loues, a Greek peasant, finishes all by himself over the actual course covered by the Greek hero Pheidippides in 490 B.C. from the battlefield of Marathon.) The ancient Olympic games, held continuously for nearly 1,200 years, passed out of existence in 394 A.D. They were revived due to the efforts of Baron Pierre de Coubertin, who conceived the plan for their rebirth.

On these two pages are four people associated with sports whose names have become a part of American slang. On the left is Steve Brodie, a Bowery character whose famous leap from the Brooklyn Bridge made news in grandpa's day. To "take a Brodie" means to take a fall. The phrase is used by the lovelorn as well as by fight fans in describing a fake knockout. Below is Annie Oakley, crack marksman of the '80's, who shot holes in playing cards. Since a free ticket is generally punctured with holes (so it won't be tallied with the receipts) a pass on the house, or anything free, is often known as an Annie Oakley.

Edward H. (Snapper) Garrison gets credit in some quarters for introducing the short stirrups and monkey crouch although Tod Sloan, who rode at the same time, is more often thought of as the originator. Garrison is still remembered by oldtimers for his spectacular finishes when he was riding high in the '80's and '90's. His specialty was coming from behind. Hence, any come-from-behind winning finish is known as a Garrison finish. The phrase was originally confined to the turf but as Garrison's fame grew it was applied to any sport. A football team, for instance, which stages a last-minute rally to win puts on a Garrison finish. It is not used now-a-days as much as it was a generation ago but most any sports fan over forty knows what a Garrison finish means.

Norman Selby, whose ring name was Kid McCoy, enriched American slang by demonstrating in a bar one evening that he was the real McCoy. Around the turn of the century, the story goes, a barfly was cadging free drinks along Broadway by claiming that he was McCoy, the fighter who had once held the welterweight and middleweight titles. Word got to the Kid about the impostor. He encountered the phony McCoy in a bar in the act of describing one of his battles to the patrons. "You're not McCoy, I am," said the Kid and straightway flattened the other man. "That guy," said the bartender pointing to the erect McCoy, "must be the real McCoy." The expression now means the real thing, the genuine article—not a substitute. One authority on slang believes that the phrase stems from the Portuguese colony, Macao, a port noted for the high quality of its uncut heroin. To a dope addict the real Macao means the best stuff obtainable. From Macao came McCoy, is the claim. But to sporting men it was the Kid, the real McCoy, who gave us the phrase.

"Rinking" became such a popular Sabbath pastime in the '80's that church attendance fell off and preachers thundered against it. On the left, a cartoonist offers a solution. The caption reads, "A hint to pastors with slim congregations on how to fill their churches."

A sports phenomenon growing out of the roller-skating fad was the birth of roller polo, a sort of ice hockey on wheels. It was a fast, action-packed game which had a tremendous following in New England and the Middle West, where it was played professionally for over twenty years. The "puck" was a solid rubber ball about the size of a tennis ball, and the players whacked it with thick curved sticks. There were five men on a side. At one time several professional leagues were in existence, but the game lost favor when the roller-skating fad began to die out in the late '90's.

One of the crack bike racers of his day was Charles (Mile-a-Minute) Murphy, whose name was famous in the '90's, when the whole country went wheeling and six-day racing was the rage. Murphy believed he could pedal a paced mile in better than a minute. He got the Long Island Railroad to build a three-mile wooden track between the rails over a level stretch on Hempstead Plains. The rear car was fitted with a hood behind which Murphy was to ride for protection against the rush of air displaced by the locomotive. After a preliminary test, Murphy took off on June 30, 1899. The engine gathered speed slowly, but when the marked mile was reached it was going an even sixty. Murphy clung to the car for the whole mile and then dropped back when the signal was given him that the mile had been passed. The engineer applied the brakes gently, and, at another signal, Murphy caught up with the train and was hauled, bike and all, aboard the car. Then the clockers conferred and announced the astonishing time: 57 ⅘ seconds. Murphy became famous overnight. He toured the country as a vaudeville headliner. Later he retired from cycling to join the New York City Police Force. He died in 1950 at the age of 79.

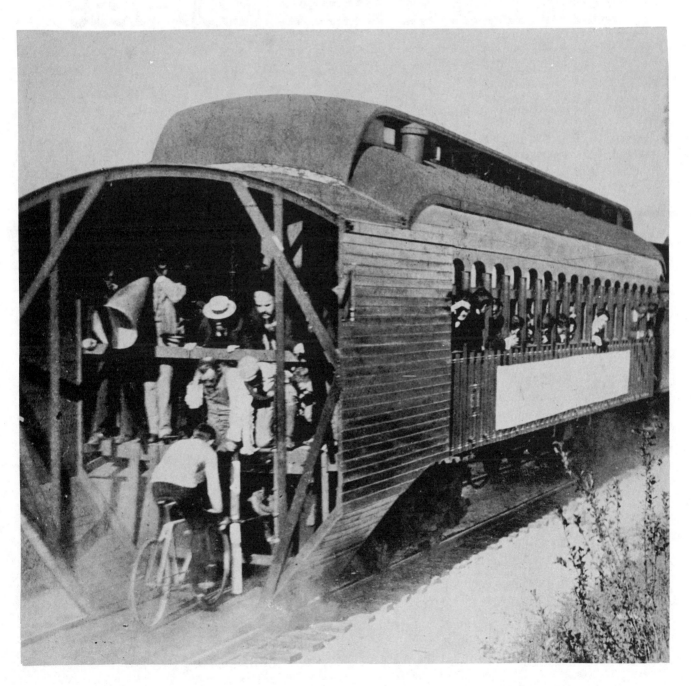

CHAPTER THREE

The Rise of Sports 1900–1918

The gas-lit era was the heyday of the founding fathers of sport, a period of development and organization, and the beginning of large-scale attendance at sporting events. Yet when the era ended (call it 1900), there were comparatively few sports that would be recognized today. A glance at the sporting picture in 1900 is revealing.

At that time there were two sports, now played and watched by millions, which were looked upon with suspicion by most people and played by relatively few. They were golf and tennis.

True, the divot-digging game was then spreading like wildfire (from 50 golf clubs in 1895 to 1,040 by 1900), but it was largely a rich-man's leisurely sport appealing to older people. Most courses were still in the cow-pasture stage, and the Britishers owned the game. In 1900, Harry Vardon, from the Isle of Jersey, won the seventh U.S. Open. An American-born player was not to win it until 1911.

The stronghold of tennis, like golf, was in the East, where it was almost exclusively the property of people of means. All the early national champions were Easterners. The game was given some popular impetus in 1900, however, when Dwight W. Davis, a Harvard student, donated a cup for annual competition among all nations. At first England and the U.S. were the only contenders.

Baseball in 1900 was creaking along after a costly war between the Players' League and the National League which nearly wrecked the game. The American League had not yet been born. Its formation in 1901 touched off another bitter battle, which lasted until 1903, when the first World Series was played.

Boxing had gained little respectability by putting on gloves. Outlawed in most states, it was without control or supervision. There were no boxing commissions in 1900. The heavyweight champion that year was Jim Jeffries, who won the crown by knocking out the 37-year-old title-holder, Bob Fitzsimmons, before a few hundred fans in a bout at Coney Island on June 9, 1899. Jeffries, believe it or not, had fought only ten times before meeting Fitzsimmons.

Football, still dominated by the Big Three, was a push-and-pull business based on power and brawn. The forward pass, and with it the open game, was yet to come.

Virtually all of our sports in 1900 were just emerging from swaddling clothes. For example, basketball was only eight years old; most speed swimmers used the side stroke; track athletes won Olympic titles in times that schoolboys would scoff at today; and horse racing was about to see a reform wave which would shut down every track in the country except those in Kentucky and Maryland.

Sports had come a long way between the Civil War and 1900, but their development in this period was nothing compared to the strides that would be taken after the turn of the century.

Whether the New-York-to-Paris auto race of 1908 should be listed as a sporting event or as a pioneering expedition is debatable. At any rate, it was an extraordinary event. Six cars left Times Square on February 12, 1908, before cheering thousands to make their way across the continent and then, after a sea voyage, to Japan and Vladivostok, across Siberia and Europe to Paris. The French entered three cars, the Italians, Germans, and Americans, one each. One by one the cars dropped out (first withdrawal was at Peekskill, New York, the day of the start) until the Americans and the Germans were the only contenders. The American-made Thomas Flyer (above), shown shortly after its start in New York, reached Paris on July 31, four days behind the Germans, but was declared the official winner by 26 days because of a handicap imposed on the other car. The Americans had covered a total of 13,341 land miles in 170 days to win the trophy.

Road racing got its start in this country when William K. Vanderbilt, Jr., put up a cup in 1904 for the winner of a 284-mile auto race to be held on Long Island. Foreign cars were then the best, and Vanderbilt, who had driven in European road races, hoped to stimulate interest in American-made cars. He did more than that. The Vanderbilt Cup Races, held on Long Island from 1904 to 1910, drew uncontrollable crowds numbering up to 500,000, as well as the fastest cars in the world. (Left, a typical contender for the Cup. Below, racing enthusiasts seek position along the course on the afternoon before the early-morning start.) The old busses turned in remarkable times over the twisting, winding course and uneven road surface. Some got up to 100 miles an hour on the straightaways. In 1908, George Robertson, an American, averaged 64 m.p.h. driving a Locomobile on a 258-mile course. His victory gave the American auto industry a tremendous impetus.

The picture below, taken on Memorial Day, 1911, shows the start of the first Indianapolis Speedway Race. Here, the cars have been cranked (note the mechanic on the far right), and the drivers sit at the steering wheels, which are on the right in this line of cars. Work on the Indianapolis Speedway began in 1909 as a result of the tremendous interest in the Vanderbilt Cup Races, and the first 500-mile test was held two years later. Since then the race has been held every year (barring the war years), and today it draws more spectators than any other single sporting event in the world. Each year between 250,000 and 300,000 people storm Indianapolis and turn the city upside down. The race has been criticized by many who say that it is a bloody spectacle, that the chance of seeing some driver crash to his death is the only thing that brings out the mob. Its supporters maintain that it is a proving ground for new ideas.

Above is Ray Harroun flashing down the home stretch in his Marmon Wasp to win the first Indianapolis. Harroun used a rear-view mirror and rode alone. He averaged 74.59 m.p.h. around the two-

and-a-half-mile track. In 1952 Troy Ruttman, a 22 year old Californian weighing 245 pounds, drove his Agajanian Special to victory with a new mark of 128.922 m.p.h. Racing experts wrongly thought in 1952 that this speed was near the absolute limit.

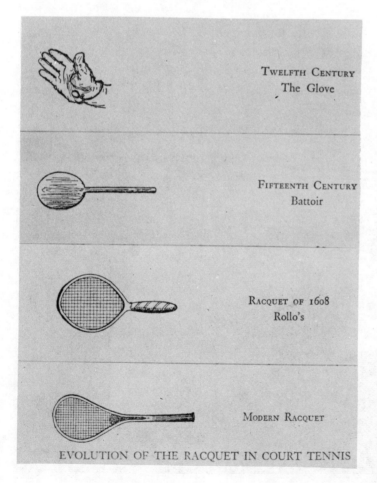

TWELFTH CENTURY
The Glove

FIFTEENTH CENTURY
Battoir

RACQUET OF 1608
Rollo's

MODERN RACQUET

EVOLUTION OF THE RACQUET IN COURT TENNIS

Court tennis is the most complicated game in the world and, in the opinion of experts and the few hundred men who play it in this country, it is the best game ever devised. Allison Danzig, of the *New York Times*, an authority on court games, says: "It is a game of moving chess, combining the exactitude of billiards, the coordination of hand and eye of lawn tennis, and the generalship and quick judgment of polo. It is not only the sum of ball games. It is the absolute in games."

The proper name of court tennis (also called "real tennis") is simply "tennis," and the common outdoor game is "lawn tennis," but by popular usage the latter has become known as "tennis." It merits description on these two pages because it is not only the oldest game played with a bat and a ball; it is also the ancestor of all court and racquet games—racquets, squash racquets, squash tennis, lawn tennis, badminton, paddle tennis, and table tennis. It is the original court game and it is played today almost exactly as it was in the Middle Ages.

The court is a reproduction of the inner court-yard of a monastery where monks first played the game in France. Longer and wider than a lawn-tennis court, the cement-walled court has a roof running along three sides. Under the roof (penthouse) are openings of various sizes. A ball hit in some of them wins a point; in others it may mean a standoff or even the loss of a point. On one side is a sheer wall (on the left in the picture). A high, sloping net divides the court, whose two sides are not at all similar, except in the dimensions of the floor. A heavily strung racket is used because the ball is solid although flannel covered. The racket has a lop-sided head, which helps put a cut on the ball, for it is a game of carom shots, baffling angles, and placement rather than a slam-bang affair. The scoring is similar to lawn tennis, and the basic idea of the two games is the same—to get the ball over the net into the other fellow's court. It can be hit against any of the four walls (sometimes two or three in one shot), it may go into one of the many openings, it may run along the roof for a while, or it may go directly across the net as in lawn tennis. Anything goes. A unique feature of the game is that one court (the far one in the picture) is always the service court. The server stays there until the receiver gets him out by making certain points against him. Then they change courts and the other player keeps serving until *he's* put out. But it's possible to lose or win points in either court. Another feature that defies description is the "chase," which is the essence of the game. It is, in effect, a point to be played over again, a suspended point, and it has to do with where the ball falls on the second bounce without being touched. Parallel lines a yard apart on the surface of the court help the marker (far right) determine exactly where the ball falls to establish the chase. The players then switch courts (a chase means loss of service) and play off the chase for the point. Here is where quick judgment and head work come in, for the conditions of the game are such that a man can win the chase by *not* hitting the ball or he can lose it *by* hitting it, and vice versa. (Complicated? So is court tennis.) There are less than a dozen courts in this country, about the same number in France, and some twenty in England. A court costs over $100,000 to build, and, were it not for this high cost, the game would probably be one of the most popular of all, for, despite its complexities, it is the one game that has everything.

One of the fastest and most exhausting games played on foot is the game of racquets, sometimes called hard racquets. It is also one of the most dangerous because of the terrific speed of the ball, which rockets off the walls faster than a line drive from a baseball player's bat. The ball is a miniature baseball, tightly wound, leather covered, and smaller than a golf ball. The court is made of a cement composition and is sixty feet long, thirty feet wide, and at least thirty feet high—about four times as large in floor area as a squash racquets court.

The game of racquets, now as exclusive as court tennis, is the ancestor of squash racquets and squash tennis, both of which are condensed versions of the original game. For a game that is limited to a few well-to-do clubs, racquets had a mean beginning. It was developed by the inmates of the Fleet Street Prison, London, in the eighteenth century. This prison was more or less a gentleman's jail, being limited to debtors rather than hardened criminals, and the inmates were allowed outdoor recesses. Among them, in all probability, were many court tennis players. They made use of the walls surrounding the prison courtyard by batting a ball against them, and thus it was that racquets began. The game came to this country by way of Canada in the middle of the last century.

The game of squash racquets is generally believed to have started at Harrow School, England, about 1850. (The above picture shows Harrow schoolboys playing the game on an outdoor court.) The boys adopted the basic principles of racquets but used a soft ball, which gave a "squashy" sound when it hit a wall. Hence the name "squash." The sport found its way to this side of the Atlantic in the 1880's. Sometime later, a lawn tennis ball and racket were tried by players who thought the semi-solid squash ball was not lively enough. The new game, which found favor in a few large Eastern cities, was called squash tennis.

To sum up the four indoor racket and court games:

Court tennis: the original net game and the only wall game employing a net.

Racquets: Ancestor of the squash games, played with a hard ball. Fifteen points constitutes a game.

Squash Racquets: By far the most popular of the indoor court games, an international sport played by men and women (above) on a wooden court—a condensation of hard racquets. The scoring is similar to the older game; the racket is a light, long-handled implement, but the ball is semi-solid and far less lively than the one used in hard racquets.

Squash Tennis: An American adaptation of squash racquets, played on the same wooden court, similar in scoring, but employing an inflated ball and a racket resembling a lawn-tennis bat. The lively ball generally rebounds to the center of the court, and a player does not have to move far to retrieve it. This game is largely confined to New York City and a few other metropolitan areas.

Here Fielding Yost points to his own picture, taken years before, when his famous point-a-minute Michigan team won the first Rose Bowl game on January 1, 1902, defeating Stanford, 49 to 0. Yost's 1901–1905 teams were the first of many great Mid-Western teams to come. In that period Michigan won 55 games, lost one, tied one, and scored a total of 2,821 points for an average of 50 points a game. They met twenty-three opponents and held them to an average of less than a point a game.

Willie Heston (left) was Yost's star halfback and the first Michigan player to make Walter Camp's All-America team. Another great was Adolph "Germany" Schulz, a 240-pound center who was faster than most backs. Experts still rank him among the very best.

In the early 1900's football was on the defensive, and by 1905 the game came close to going overboard. In that season alone eighteen players were killed and more than 150 were seriously injured. (Today there are at least twenty times more college footballers than there were then, and there are far fewer injuries and deaths. Most fatalities are limited to untrained sand-lotters and high school boys.) Shove-and-pull mass plays by their very nature produced slugging, injuries and poor sportsmanship.

(Below, left and right: a power play at the goal, an injured player untended while the game goes on.) President Theodore Roosevelt, a strong advocate of vigorous athletics, realized that the game would pass out of existence unless something were done. In October, 1905, he summoned representatives of Harvard, Yale, and Princeton to the White House and demanded that the game be freed of brutality and foul play. The result was the formation of the American Football Rules Committee, and the introduction in 1906 of plays designed to open up the game. The distance to be gained on the final down was changed from five yards to ten, and the forward pass was allowed. With these revolutionary changes eligibility rules were tightened to discourage the tramp athlete, then in his heyday. The Western Conference led the way by imposing the three-year playing rule. The Big Three barred freshmen from varsity competition and demanded a year's residence for transfers. The reforms did not open up the game immediately as there were too many restrictions on the forward pass, but they led the way to a faster and less brutal game.

As revolutionary as the reforms of 1906 was the appearance of the full-time coach, making the job his life's work. The game which "belonged to the boys" before the turn of the century now was taken over by the salaried specialist. The pioneer of the new order was Amos Alonzo Stagg (above), who, as a young Yale graduate, came to the University of Chicago in 1892 and spent the next forty-one years there as football coach and athletic director. The "Grand Old Man of Football" is considered the greatest inventor of plays, among them ends back, fake kickoff, backfield shift, quick kick and double pass with forward pass. Stagg coached football for seventy years. On August 16, 1962 he celebrated his hundredth birthday and was toasted by 10,000 Americans across the country. He died in 1965.

Another inventive genius was Glenn S. (Pop) Warner, captain of the 1894 Cornell team. Warner turned out great teams at Carlisle, Pittsburgh, and Stanford. He is credited with originating the crouch start, the clipping block, and the single and double wing-back formations. Warner was the trickiest and most imaginative of all coaches.

A most remarkable coach was Gilmore Dobie (right), known as "Gloomy Gil" because of his sour-apple personality. Gil was Minnesota's quarterback at the turn of the century. He began coaching at North Dakota Agricultural in 1906. He was there two years, then went to Washington and coached the Huskies from 1908 to 1916. He did not lose a game at either place. His string of eleven seasons without a loss has yet to be beaten. Gil came east in 1917 and turned out fine teams at Navy and Cornell. Under his iron hand Cornell was unbeaten three years (1921–23).

Percy Haughton (below) was Harvard's first paid coach, and under him the Crimson knew its glory days. His 1908, 1910, 1912, 1913, and 1914 teams were undefeated, and during his regime (1908-1918) Harvard lost only seven games. Haughton was a disciplinarian and a perfectionist. The "Haughton System," based on precision and deception, stressed the hidden ball, screened lateral passes, and intricate forward-pass formations.

Lines running parallel to the sidelines at five-yard intervals made the gridiron look like a checkerboard in 1906. The longitudinal lines assisted the officials in seeing that the man taking the center pass did not hit the line within five yards of center. He was not allowed to cross the line within that area, the idea being to discourage mass plays through center. Nor could a forward pass be thrown within five yards of center.

One of the oldest of the traditional college football trophies is the "Little Brown Jug" for which Michigan and Minnesota battle annually. Since 1903, when a Minnesota student grabbed the jug after the Michigan game, it has changed hands many times. Traditional games were no longer an Eastern property by that time. Intense rivalries had developed in the Middle West and on the Pacific Coast before the turn of the century.

Football, which has become less and less of a kicking game, saw its last great toe artist in Charlie Brickley, Harvard captain in 1914. Brickley was an able ball-carrier, a deadly blocker and tackler, and, on top of that, had the most educated toe ever seen. Brickley (shown above after his Harvard days) kicked thirty-four field goals, most of them drop kicks, for Harvard in his three-year career. (It was actually two years, for he was stricken with appendicitis and saw little action in his last year.) Almost any time Brickley was inside the fifty-yard line, he was good for three points. And he could split the cross bar from any angle. His greatest performance was in the 1913 Yale game, when he booted five goals to defeat the Elis 15 to 5. Brickley made Camp's All-America team for two years. He was never on a losing team at Cambridge. Eddie Mahan and Tack Hardwick, among Harvard's best, were his team mates, but it is doubtful if the Crimson could have won them all without Brickley. He beat Dartmouth, 3-0, in 1912 and in the next year won the Princeton game, 3-0.

On the left is the Harvard Stadium, which was, at the time of its dedication on November 14, 1903, the largest reinforced-steel structure in the world, and America's first football stadium. The Harvards started something when they went in for attendance on the grand scale. Yale followed with the Bowl and Princeton with the Palmer Stadium in 1914. Within a few years the old wooden stands were as outmoded in the larger colleges as the prairie schooner. Above is a typical crowd at an Army-Navy game in pre-stadium days.

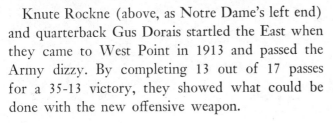

Knute Rockne (above, as Notre Dame's left end) and quarterback Gus Dorais startled the East when they came to West Point in 1913 and passed the Army dizzy. By completing 13 out of 17 passes for a 35-13 victory, they showed what could be done with the new offensive weapon.

The forward pass was not brand new in 1913. It had been permitted since 1906, but it was hampered by many restrictions. For example, if the ball hit the ground before being touched by a player of either side, the offensive team lost the ball; and a pass completed over the goal line was a touchback for the defending team. Even with these restrictions, the pass was used on occasion. Navy beat Army, 10-0, in 1906 by means of the pass; Yale threw five passes in the Wesleyan game that year and completed none. The old power game was good enough, Easterners believed. The pass was a bit unmanly. The 1910 season saw the most important rule changes since the reforms of 1906. To eliminate mass plays forever, seven men were required to be on the scrimmage line, interlocking interference was outlawed, and, for the first time, the back who first handled the ball on the snapback could cross the scrimmage line at any point. More important, forward passes could be thrown across the line at any point. The game was opening up. The pass had come into its own, but the East still was suspicious of it, even after Rockne and Dorais showed how the overhead weapon could be used.

In 1875, James Gordon Bennett, Jr., an American sportsman who had seen polo played at the Hurlingham Club in England, returned to this country with a supply of polo mallets and balls and a determination to introduce the game here. His friends became interested enough to order a carload of cow ponies from Texas and train them. As a result the game got under way in New York City in 1876. The next summer several matches were played at the Jerome Park Race Course. The sport spread to Long Island, Westchester, and Newport within the next few years, and in 1886 a picked American team challenged the Hurlingham Club to a match.

The picture below is an artist's conception of the first international polo match, played at Newport on August 25, 1886. Note the midget-size ponies, so small that the players seem to be dragging their feet on the ground. The ponies weren't that tiny, but they were not as large as today's breed. The more experienced Britishers won easily, two games to none for the Americans.

Not until 1909, when the Big Four was organized, did the Americans see victory. The quartet above, composed (from left to right) of Devereux Milburn, Harry Payne Whitney, Monty Waterbury, and Larry Waterbury, was the first American team to lift the international cup. An amazed British crowd saw this hard-hitting, rough-riding quartet overwhelm England's best. The reckless American style was nothing like the English game, which was conservative, based on superb horsemanship and short, snappy passes. The American game caused many spills (the picture, right, shows a player who has just been dumped) and the U.S.A. team was criticized by some Britishers for its rough tactics. It was Milburn primarily who devised the revolutionary American game, which has since been adopted by poloists the world over.

A year after Fitzsimmons won the title, a young giant from San Francisco named James J. Jeffries came to New York for his first Eastern appearance. Jeffries had been Corbett's sparring partner at Carson City and not much was thought of him. He looked slow and clumsy in the training camp. But he was big. (Jeff stood six feet, 1½ inches, and weighed 210 pounds in fighting trim.) Tommy Ryan, a shrewd boxing teacher, liked his looks and thought something could be done with the amiable giant. Ryan taught him to use a crouch and move in with his beamlike left arm extended. With this stance, later to become famous as the "Jeffries crouch," the big fellow was as impenetrable as a tank. He won a few fights on the West Coast and then fought Fitzsimmons for the title. Employing the crouch, the green youngster wore down the old champion and knocked him out in the eleventh round. A few months later Jeffries outpointed Tom Sharkey (below, Sharkey facing the camera) in a twenty-five-round bout. Sharkey was a tough, squat battler who had the misfortune to appear when there were many great heavyweights on the scene. He fought them all but could never quite win the crown.

One of the ring's most remarkable gladiators was Bob Fitzsimmons (above). Fitzsimmons was knock-kneed and ungainly, but had abnormally broad shoulders and long, dangling arms. John L. Sullivan described him as "a fighting machine on stilts." Ruby Bob (his scant hair was red, and he was covered with freckles) was born in Cornwall, England, grew up in New Zealand, and came to this country in 1890. A year later he knocked out the original Jack Dempsey to win the world middleweight title. Fitzsimmons ran up a string of knockouts thereafter. On March 17, 1897, Fitz, who was then 34 years old and weighed 156½ pounds, met Corbett at Carson City, Nevada, for the world's heavyweight championship. To the astonishment of almost everyone, the older and lighter challenger flattened Corbett, the master boxer, in the fourteenth round.

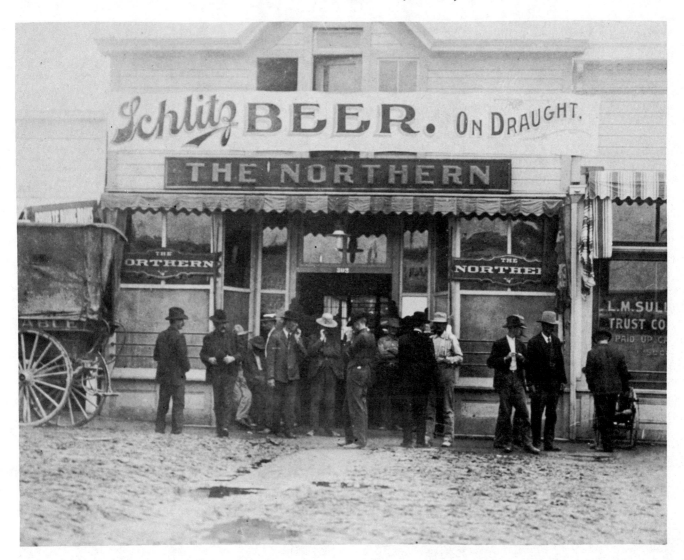

When Jeffries was at his zenith, one of the greatest little men the ring has ever seen appeared in the person of Joe Gans, a Baltimore Negro. Gans was such a great boxer and hitter that he was hailed as "The Old Master" by his contemporaries. He was so good that to get fights he sometimes had to agree to lose and, even as lightweight champion, to take the short end of the purse. His last great performance was against Battling Nelson at Goldfield, Nevada, on September 3, 1906, in Tex Rickard's first promotional venture. Rickard owned the Northern Saloon (above) and displayed the $34,000 purse in gold coins in the window. (Right, Nelson fondles the coins.) Nelson took the major share of the purse and also a fine shellacking.

This is a picture of Jim Jeffries as he looked in 1910, when he was thirty-five-years old. He bears little resemblance to the rugged, black-haired youngster who lifted Bob Fitzsimmon's crown at Coney Island eleven years before. After the battle, Jeff announced that he was going to be a fighting champion—and he was. Unlike Corbett, who fought few bouts as champion, Jeff put his title on the line any time anyone deserved a crack at it. After the Sharkey bout, he gave Corbett a chance to regain the title. Corbett still thought of Jeffries as a sparring partner, and for twenty-two rounds the champion looked it. But in the twenty-third round, with only two more to go and victory certain for Corbett if he stayed on his feet, Jeff caught his old boss coming off the ropes and smashed him to the canvas. Jeff kept on putting up his title. He defended it three times in 1901, flattened Fitzsimmons again the following year, and Corbett for the second time in 1903. When Jeff knocked out Jack Munroe in two rounds a year later he announced that he was through. There was nobody left to fight. For six years Jeffries did not step inside the ropes. Meanwhile Jack Johnson, a Negro from Galveston, Texas, had come to the fore, and Jeffries' admirers, who believed the retired champion invincible, persuaded him to have it out with Johnson—for the honor of the white race, as the cry was. Tex Rickard (above) acted as promoter and referee. The bout took place at Reno, Nevada, on July 4, 1910.

Jack Johnson (shown above examining the purse for the Jeffries battle as Rickard—far left—watches) won the heavyweight title by stopping Tommy Burns in fourteen rounds in a bout held near Sydney, Australia, on December 26, 1908. Burns was at that time the accepted champion, the best of a mediocre lot following Jeff's retirement. But when he met Johnson he looked like anything but a champion. The big Negro with the hairless ebony head and golden teeth toyed with the white man, taunted him throughout the bout, and hit him at will. There was no denying Johnson's ability. He was a superb boxer with a punishing blow in either hand and was amazingly fast for a big man. He was always in a position to hit, never off balance, and he was a master of the art of feinting. Many consider Johnson the best heavyweight of all time with Jeffries in his prime a close second. But Jeff was not in his prime when he met Johnson. He had been out of the ring so long that he was rusty and flabby. He had to take off almost 75 pounds to make 227 pounds, his weight when he climbed through the ropes at Reno.

The fight had not gone two rounds before it was apparent to everyone in the crowd that Jeffries had nothing. The once-great fighter kept shuffling forward in his famous crouch trying to break through Johnson's defense. The colored man smothered him, jolted him with a series of short uppercuts, and poured forth a stream of offensive chatter. (Here, Jeffries in his crouch vainly tries to reach Johnson's midsection as the colored man taunts him.) Johnson boxed cautiously at first, but as the fight wore on and he saw that he had nothing to fear from the bewildered, stumbling Jeffries, he opened up and went after his man. Hitting him almost at will from the tenth round on, Johnson was unable to put him down until the fifteenth. A long left to the jaw did it. Jeff went down slowly, got up at ten, and then went down again. Once more he painfully got to his feet. Johnson rushed him across the ring throwing rights and lefts. Jeff collapsed in a heap and his seconds threw in the sponge. After the fight, Johnson, who was wanted on a charge of violating the Mann Act (a Federal morals offense), fled the country.

Now began a search for a White Hope to whip the Negro for the honor of the Caucasian race. Of the many who appeared, the most impressive was Jess Willard, a Kansas cowboy who knew nothing about fighting but was so enormous that on size alone he might have a chance against Johnson. Willard weighed 240 pounds and was six feet, seven inches tall. While the Kansan was pushing over a number of second-raters in the East, Johnson was broke and ring-rusty in Europe. A juicy offer to defend his title against Willard lured him to Havana, where, on April 5, 1915, with his third white wife in the stands, he succumbed to age, fat, and Willard's blows in the twenty-sixth round. (The picture above shows the Negro taking the count; right, a non-ferocious-looking Willard.)

Byron Bancroft (Ban) Johnson announced in 1900 that the Western League, which he had successfully operated for a number of years, was now the American League, equal to the National in status. (Johnson stands on the right of the two figures in this picture.) Johnson's announcement touched off a two-year war with the National League, from which he emerged the winner.

Johnson, a former sports writer with executive ability, had a lot of new ideas for the fledgling circuit. One of them was his insistence on full authority and protection for his umpires. (The cartoon below, drawn in 1900, offers a solution for the National League umpires who were harassed by fans and intimidated by club owners.) Johnson standardized their uniforms and saw to it that their decisions were backed up by the League.

Johnson raided the older league, grabbed some thirty stars, and annexed Washington and Cleveland, which had been National League cities for ten years. One of the key figures in the game during the war between the two leagues was Connie Mack (right), manager of the Milwaukee club. Johnson persuaded Mack to bring his club to Philadelphia in 1901, the first year the American League took the field, and battle the Phillies for patronage. John McGraw predicted that the club would be the "White Elephant" of the American League. But Connie Mack's team was to survive and equal the achievements of McGraw's Giants. When Mack retired, in October, 1951, it marked the end of a sixty-five-year major-league career, fifty of those years spent as manager of the Athletics.

If there ever was any question about baseball being the national pastime, there was none after President William Howard Taft (above) threw out the first ball to open the 1910 season. Taft made it official, and every president since then has honored the game in like manner. The most enthusiastic fans among the presidents were Taft, Woodrow Wilson, Warren G. Harding, Herbert C. Hoover and John F. Kennedy.

Ty Cobb's name led all the rest in his flaming twenty-four-year career as an American League star —and it still leads all the rest in almost every branch of the game—in most hits made (4,191), most games played (3,033), most runs scored (2,244), most stolen bases (892), and the highest lifetime batting average (.367). He was a whirlwind on the base paths, the most feared base-runner of them all. (Here, he rounds third, with the tip of his toe just touching a corner of the sack.) In one season, 1915, he stole 96 bases, a record that stood for forty-two years, until the Dodger shortstop, Maury Wills, stole 104 (in a 162-game season). Cobb's record was made when the clubs played 154 games a season.

This is Cobb coming home, the way he came into every base—at full speed and feet first. "The base paths belong to the runner," said Cobb. "If anyone blocks my way I'll cut him to ribbons." He was so antagonistic and bitterly competitive that he was detested by all who opposed him, even by his own teammates, who were jealous of his personal glory. He fought with umpires, players, and fans. Every game was a World Series contest to Cobb. He never quit. One September morning, when the Tigers were in New York to play the Yankees in a series that meant nothing in the pennant race, Grantland Rice called on the star at his hotel. He found him in bed with a temperature of 102°, and legs taped from ankle to thigh. He was crippled enough to be in a hospital. That afternoon Rice watched Cobb get three hits, steal two bases, and win the game by himself. Cobb was a perfectionist, a tireless student of the game. He originated the idea of wearing weighted shoes in training and switching to lighter ones when the season opened. He was the first to swing three bats before taking his turn at the plate. In his long major-league career (Detroit, 1905–1926; Athletics, 1927–1928) he hit over .400 three times and was batting champion for twelve years. Cobb was the game's greatest genius and its keenest mind.

Napoleon (Larry) Lajoie switched from the National to the American League when the new circuit was formed to become its most popular player. A big, friendly man, Larry was the Adonis of the diamond—and he was good, too. He played second for Cleveland, where he hit over .300 for eleven years and one year topped .400. He is remembered more for his fielding, his flawless skill in handling the ball. Larry had the gift of making everything look easy. He was the most graceful of all infielders.

No pitcher ever had as much control as Christy Mathewson. Grover Hartley, one of his catchers, said that Matty could throw a fast ball, curve, or fadeaway into an area the size of a grapefruit any time he wanted to. He didn't care much about strike-outs; he'd let the batters pop up or hit into the dirt and be thrown out. And he was the stingiest pitcher in giving a base on balls. In 1908 he pitched 56 games and walked only 42 batters. Matty was one of the first college athletes to play big-league ball. He went from Bucknell University to the Giants in 1900 and stayed until 1916, when he went to Cincinnati as manager. His most phenomenal feat was his three straight shutouts of the A's in the 1905 World Series. He won thirty or more games for three seasons, better than twenty a season for twelve consecutive years.

Bill Dinneen, an American League umpire for twenty-eight years, used to say of Walter Johnson, "Nobody could ever throw a baseball as fast as Johnson." Baseball men agree that of the standout fireballers—Feller, Grove, and Dean—Johnson was the fastest. Washington was a second-division team during most of the twenty-one years (1907–1927) Johnson served there, but, despite its lowly position, he managed to win 414 games. The big, soft-spoken Kansan relied on speed and control and, when he had two strikes on a batter, a curve that was nothing more than a wrinkle. Smart hitters like Cobb and Eddie Collins used to take two strikes and wait for the so-called curve. Only so could they hit him. Effortless delivery enabled Johnson to keep going until he was forty, an age when most fireballers are through.

Whenever baseball experts select an all-time, all-star team they are always in agreement on the shortstop—John Peter Wagner, known as Hans. There is no one else. His record doesn't match Cobb's or Ruth's, perhaps, but as an all-around team player he is unequaled. The Dutchman, who wore a Pirate uniform for eighteen years (1900–1917), could play any position on the field and play it well. John McGraw said of him, "He was a fine catcher, as good a third baseman as I ever saw, one of the best outfielders, the best shortstop, and one of the greatest hitters." Ed Barrow, the architect of the New York Yankees, always maintained that the Dutchman was the best of them all, including Cobb and Ruth. So

did McGraw. Wagner was bow-legged and awkward and had a pair of gorillalike arms. But he was fast and covered a wide range. With hands like shovels, he could scoop up anything in sight and rifle the ball to any base. On the base paths he was almost as good as Cobb (720 stolen bases), and he was never known to slash a blocking baseman. He was mild-mannered and sportsmanlike at all times and rarely beefed at an umpire. A powerful hitter—he weighed 200 pounds and had tremendous shoulders—Wagner didn't slip below .300 until he was forty years old, in 1914. He led the National League in batting eight times, in homers seven times, and for seventeen consecutive years hit .300 or better. The Dutchman was good.

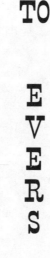

The Cubs' great triumvirate, Joe Tinker, Johnny Evers, and Frank Chance, brought glory and four pennants to Chicago in the first decade of the century. The three scrappy youngsters first got together in 1902 and immediately captured the imagination of baseball fans and sports writers with their aggressive, heads-up brand of ball. They were the snappiest double-play artists of the time, and their fame spread when Franklin P. Adams wrote:

These are the saddest of possible words:
"Tinker to Evers to Chance."
Trio of Bear Cubs and fleeter than birds,
"Tinker to Evers to Chance."
Ruthlessly pricking our gonfalon bubble,
Making a Giant hit into a double,
Words that are weighty with nothing but trouble—
"Tinker to Evers to Chance."

Adams was a New York newspaper columnist when he wrote the eight-line lament, and his grief was shared by all Giant fans. Joe Tinker, at shortstop, was a stocky, bull-necked battler, and the oldest of the trio. He was twenty-two in 1902. Johnny Evers, a lantern-jawed midget weighing 125 pounds, was only nineteen. He was the middle man. On first was Frank Chance, twenty-one years old. The three kids were high-strung, individualistic, and full of fight. They battled umpires, players, and each other—Evers and Tinker didn't speak off the field for years—but they worked with consummate smoothness on the diamond. There was more to the team than the three youngsters. Johnny Kling, the backstop, was one of the best, and on the mound were Ed Reulbach, Jack Pfeister (he could always beat the Giants), and Three-Fingered Brown, whose square name was Mordecai Peter Centennial Brown. Three-Fingered lost half of the index finger of his right hand in a corn shredder when he was a lad, and the stubby digit enabled him to put a weird twist on the ball. He had superb control and was always reliable. Brown was the one pitcher who had the edge on Christy Mathewson when the two met.

Between 1904 and 1916, the two rivals clashed twenty-four times, with Brown winning thirteen of the games, nine of which came consecutively. On September 4, 1916, they faced each other for the last time, Matty winning, 10 to 8. Neither ever pitched a game after that. The Cubs won pennants in 1906, '07, '08, and '10 under the leadership of Frank Chance. The first baseman, who was playing manager (1905–1912), earned the title given him by Chicago fans—"The Peerless Leader."

George Stallings was a major-league manager for thirteen years and won only one flag, but to all baseball historians he is "The Miracle Man." (Stallings, above, sits on the bench with the three pitchers who made him the Miracle Man. From left to right: Bill James, Stallings, George Tyler, and Dick Rudolph.) An American League managerial discard, Stallings came to the Braves in 1913 and advanced them from last place to fifth. In 1914, it looked like back to the cellar for George when the Braves lost 18 of their first 22 games and were in last place as late as July 19. Then they began to move. The three hurlers caught fire and pitched superb ball day after day. The Braves moved into first place on September 5 and clinched the pennant by ten and a half games on September 29. That wasn't all. The red-hot club then took on the heavily favored Athletics, who had won three World Series in the previous four years, and walloped them in four straight games. It was the first time a team had swept a World Series. No team before had ever rocketed to such heights from such a lowly position. They were a great one-season flash combination. Stallings never repeated. The Braves dropped to second place the next year, to third in 1916, and then became a second-division fixture. Stallings was fired after the 1920 season, when the club finished seventh. But for one bright year he was the Miracle Man, and he is so remembered today.

The above scene is typical of the national tennis championships held at Newport when the game was dominated by Eastern players, most of them Harvard men. (The Harvard dynasty of singles champions —Robert D. Wrenn, F. H. Hovey, and Malcolm D. Whitman—lasted from 1893 to 1901, when William A. Larned of Cornell won the championship.) The game was beginning to change from the patty-pat stage to real tennis. The college men came up to the net, used the passing shot, the twist service, the drop shot, and the lob. It was not the slashing, aggressive game it is today, but the modern game was on the way. Gone was the underhand service (left), which was given up in the '80's when O. E. Woodhouse, an English player, dazzled Staten Islanders by introducing the overhead service.

134

This is the original Davis Cup team of 1900 (below), a Harvard trio composed of (from left to right): Malcolm D. Whitman, Davis, and Holcolmbe Ward. The British sent a team of three ranking players to this country in 1900 and to the surprise of most everybody, the Americans blanked them, 5 to 0.

The Harvard youngsters became the top tennis players of their time. Ward won the U.S. singles in 1904 and was doubles champion six times. His partner, 1899–1901, was Davis. Whitman was U.S. singles champion 1898–1900. All three lived to see the cup contested by some 25 nations.

One of the oldest contested trophies is the Davis Cup, which was put up by a young Harvard student in 1900 named Dwight F. Davis (shown above, as he looked in 1910). Davis' idea was to stimulate competition between the United States and England, to attract attention to tennis and to create a sports event to which spectators would be drawn.

Davis, who later became Secretary of War under Coolidge and Governor-General of the Philippines, little dreamed when he donated the cup that it would one day become the most widely traveled trophy in existence.

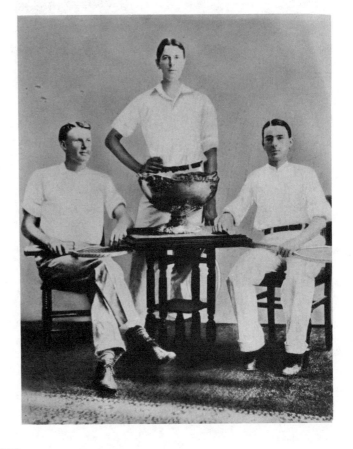

In the summer of 1914, two men from Down Under came to this country to try for the Davis Cup, which the United States had won from England the year before. They were Tony Wilding (above), of New Zealand, and Norman Brookes (above, right), of Australia—later Sir Norman Brookes. The two-man team representing Australia had beaten the United States in 1908, '09, and '11, and now, with the outbreak of World War I and with orders to return home, the great pair teamed up for the last time. (Wilding was killed during a landing at Gallipoli.) It was fitting that they should win this final time and win they did, 3 to 2, but not before one

of the greatest sets of Davis Cup history had been played by the two titans, Brookes and Maurice M. (Red) McLoughlin, the California Comet. In the first set the score mounted to 9-8 and 40-love in favor of Brookes. Then McLouglin shot over three aces to make it deuce. Then he took game and, in a nerve-racking, seesaw marathon, finally won out 17-15. The remaining two sets were easy for the redhead. Now the matches stood at two-all, but the Anzacs won the doubles and went home with the Cup. There was no Davis Cup competition during World War I. Not until 1920 did the United States regain the trophy. It remained here seven years.

When the redheaded McLoughlin came East to win the national championship at Newport in 1912, he changed the game almost overnight. What had been a cautious game of serve, stay back, lob, with an occasional venture into the forecourt, soon became a game of power serves, with dashes to the net, volleying, and passing shots down the sidelines. Nothing comparable to his style had ever been seen before. McLoughlin had dash, color, and a ready smile. Wherever he played, he was a great favorite with the crowd. At Newport, Wimbledon, and Forest Hills he was idolized. Here was an "outsider," a non-Easterner dynamiting his way to victory before ever-increasing crowds. By speeding up the game, McLoughlin awakened the country to tennis. No longer did the hoi polloi sneer at it as a sissy game.

137

The Great Old Man of golf in the early days was Walter J. Travis (above), who didn't take up the game until he was thirty-five years old. Born in Australia, Travis came here as a boy and became an American by adoption. Four years after he took his first swing at the guttie ball (1896), Travis was good enough to win the Amateur. Twice more he won the title (1901 and 1903), and then, in 1904, he went to England and took the British Amateur. This was the cup's first trip to these shores, and the event started many a middle-aged businessman on a golfing career. Travis was a short driver, but he made it up with deadly approaches and uncanny putting. As his career waned, a young man with a similar name, Jerome D. Travers, won the American Amateur four times, the Open once. For a decade the golfing world resounded with the names of these friendly rivals.

Until Johnny McDermott (above) won the American Open in 1911, the crown had gone to "foreigners" since its inception in 1894, when Willie Dunn first took it at St. Andrews and with it a $300 purse. American pros had been coming on before McDermott's triumph, but they had never quite been able to make it. In 1909, for instance, Tommy McNamara of Boston lost by a whisker, but not before he had turned in a 69 to become the first man to break 70 in a major tournament. Johnny McDermott was a wispy 130-pound caddy from Atlantic City, but there was nothing wispy about his ego. He believed and stated that he could whip any man on any course at any time and was willing to back his claim with any amount. He took the Open in 1911 and 1912 and might have reached golfing immortality had not a nervous breakdown forced him to retire

Golf was considered a man's game by the dour golfing fathers at St. Andrews, and it remained so until the Shinnecock Hills Club on Long Island let down the gates in 1891 and invited the ladies to tag along with their husbands. The girls liked the game so much that two years later they persuaded the men to lay out a separate nine-hole course for their exclusive use. This was the start. Within the next couple of years, ladies' courses were built at Morristown, New Jersey, and at Yonkers. (The latter was not on the hallowed St. Andrews grounds, where women were considered untouchables until the 1930's.) With the influx of women golfers, it was only natural that a tournament should be held, and the course chosen was the Morristown seven-holer. The winner of the two-day affair (October 17 and 18, 1894) was Miss Holland A. Ford, who scored a 94 on the double seven, defeating her nearest rival by fourteen strokes. In 1895 another women's tournament was held but it did not receive U.S.G.A. sanction. However, next year when the first match play tournament was held, the winner, Beatrice Hoyt, was officially recognized as the Women's Amateur Champion.

A GOLF WIDOW

By 1913 the United States had shown that it could hold its own against the world in all sports with the exception of golf. American competitors had done well in the Olympics and had taken England's measure in tennis, yachting, boxing, and polo. But golf was still dominated by Britishers and Scots. The world's finest golfer at the time was Harry Vardon, and right alongside him was Ted Ray. Both were English. (Vardon had won the British Open five times and was to win it again in 1914; Ray was the 1912 champion.) The two pros came to the United States in 1913 and toured the country giving exhibitions before record crowds. It was a foregone conclusion that one or the other would take the American Open, scheduled for The Country Club, Brookline, Mass., in mid-September.

Francis Ouimet (above, with his caddy, Eddie Lowery, during the play off of the 1913 Open) was a local boy, twenty years old when Vardon and Ray interrupted their tour to play at Brookline. He lived across the street from The Country Club, had caddied there as a schoolboy, and had gained minor fame in 1913 as winner of the Massachusetts State Amateur. (To be eligible he had to be a member of a recognized golf club, so Francis borrowed $25 from his mother and joined the Woodland Golf Club.) He was talked into entering the Open by Robert Watson, president of the U.S.G.A. Johnny McDermott was there to defend his title. Other stars were Jerry Travers, Macdonald Smith, Jim Barnes, and Wilfried Reid, a British pro. Louis Tellier, the French links master, was also competing. Ouimet seemed unimportant.

During the qualifying round Ouimet played his consistent unspectacular game and finished a stroke behind Vardon, who posted a total of 151. An unknown youngster named Walter Hagen, playing his first national tournament, carded 157. With the qualifying round out of the way, the championship test began—72 holes of medal play over a tough par-71 course. At the end of 54 holes, Vardon, Ray, and Ouimet were tied for the lead at 225, but no one expected the youthful amateur to weather the terrific pressure of the last round. But weather it he did, with a blazing finish, by playing the last six holes in 22 strokes (2 under par) to gain a tie with Vardon and Ray. The impossible had happened. Ouimet was carried off the eighteenth green on the shoulders of the crowd. But he still had to face the play off. Despite the rain, a gallery of 8,000 was on hand when the three teed off next day. As the round progressed and Ouimet refused to crack, it dawned on the spectators that they were witnessing one of the most momentous events in golf history. They shouted themselves hoarse as Ouimet came to the seventeenth, one stroke on top of Vardon, with Ray five strokes away. Vardon elected to try a risky drive on the 360-yard dogleg. It proved his undoing. He hooked into a bunker and had to take a five. Ouimet, straight as an arrow, picked up two strokes and now, with a three-stroke lead, realized for the first time that he was going to win. He did not let up. (Below, the eighteenth green, where Ouimet sunk his final putt for a four to win the match.) Ouimet's stunning victory has been called, "The Shots Heard Round the World." It was Ouimet who gave golf its great impetus by showing that it was a game anyone could play. Within a decade it had become all America's game. There were 350,000 golfers in 1913, more than two million ten years later. By 1964 an estimated six million golfers were playing 7,000 courses.

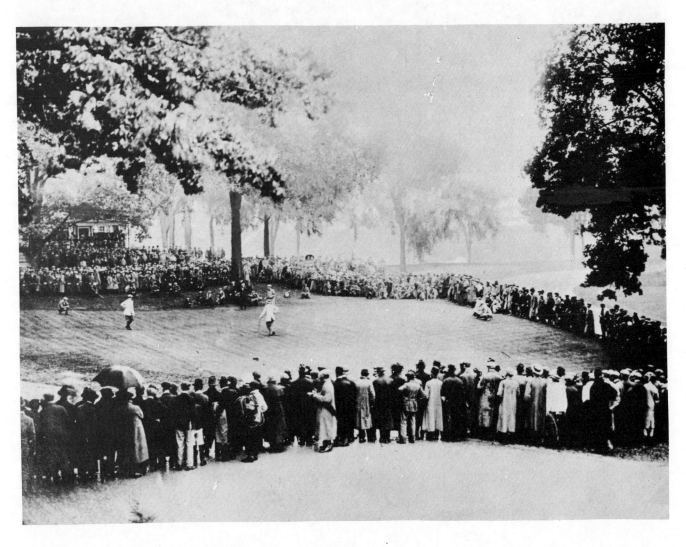

Eighty thousand people were in the huge stadium at London on July 13, 1908, waiting excitedly for the first marathon runner to come through the entrance and circle the track to the finish line. It was the Fourth Olympiad, the first big one in number of competitors, nations participating, and range of athletic events. The marathon had started at Windsor Castle, 26 miles, 385 yards away (the classic distance), and the entire course was lined with spectators. By the time the runners had come to within three miles of the stadium, the leaders were Dorando, the Italian, Hefferon, of South Africa, and the Americans Johnny Hayes and Joe Forshaw. Dorando, coming within sight of the stadium, put on a spurt to lead the field.

A mighty roar greeted the Italian as he came through the entrance. But the roar quickly died down when the crowd saw him glance dazedly around, start in the wrong direction, and then collapse. Helping hands grabbed the spent runner. He was lifted to his feet and, staggering at every step, was practically dragged across the tape. (The above picture shows the finish.) A few yards behind him came Johnny Hayes, fresh as a starting sprinter. The American finished barely half a minute behind the now-unconscious Dorando, who was promptly disqualified. Doctors worked over the Italian all afternoon and for a time despaired of his life. Johnny Hayes got the gold medal, but Queen Alexandra, who had witnessed the dramatic finish, rewarded Dorando with a special gold trophy, her own personal gift.

Jim Thorpe, the greatest all-around athlete of all time, held the spotlight at the next Olympic games, held at Stockholm in 1912. Thorpe, an American Indian, who found training a drudgery and rarely bothered to get in shape, dazzled the world by the ease with which he won the pentathlon and decathlon, the two all-around events on the program. Against a field of highly trained specialists from the world over, the big, 190-pound Indian with the perfect build won the pentathlon by taking 4 of five events with a score that was twice as good as his nearest rival's. Then he went on to win the ten-event decathlon with four first places, finishing well up in the other six events. King Gustaf V was so impressed that he gave the Indian a special trophy —a huge jeweled chalice in the shape of a Viking ship. As he presented it, the King said, "You, sir, are the greatest athlete in the world." "Thanks, King," said Jim. Misfortune followed Thorpe's triumph. Later, when it was found that he had played semi-pro ball in the summer of 1911, his gold medals and the trophy were taken from him, and his Olympic records were stricken from the books. Years later Jim's friends tried to recover his trophy but the effort failed.

If any man can be called a super-athlete it is Jim Thorpe. For more than a dozen years he was the terror of college and pro football. (Above, as a pro on the Canton Bulldogs, Jim seizes a ball carrier.) He was twice named halfback on Walter Camp's All-America teams (1911 and 1912), he was the world's all-around track champion, and he played major-league ball for six years. Forty years after Thorpe's golden days, the Associated Press conducted a poll of the nation's sports experts to determine the greatest performers in various fields of sports over the half-century. Jim was named the Greatest Male Athlete, Greatest Football Player, and took second place to Jesse Owens as the Greatest Track Performer. There will never be another Thorpe. If he had never done anything but play football he would be hailed as one of the immortals, for on the gridiron he had no peer. In more than thirty college games, the indestructible Indian never needed a time out. In his last year at Carlisle (1912), he made twenty-five touchdowns and 198 points, a scoring record still unmatched by any player.

Statistics cannot tell the story, of course. The opinion of an unbiased football analyst such as Percy Haughton is worth more than a book of figures. Haughton had a good look at Thorpe when the Carlisle Indians, coached by Pop Warner, played Harvard in 1911. Haughton, a cool, scholarly critic of the game, watched open-mouthed as the Indian shattered his line, ran wild around the ends, and pulverized the Crimson offense. Virtually single-handed, Thorpe beat a fine Harvard team. Later, Haughton said, "Watching him turn the ends, slash off tackle, kick and pass and tackle, I realized that here was the theoretical super-player in flesh and blood." Haughton was not alone in his opinion. Thorpe could do more things on a football field and do them better than anyone else. He could run with Red Grange and Doc Blanchard, smash a line like Bronco Nagurski, place kick and punt with the best—he often booted the ball eighty yards—and he was a devastating tackler and blocker. There was a popular saying, when Thorpe was dismantling such football powers as Pitt, Army, and Penn: "He could make a first down against any team in the country behind a schoolboy line." He probably could have, at that.

Before Thorpe's college career was over, five major-league ball clubs had sent offers to him through Pop Warner, his advisor. John McGraw, aware of the publicity value of the Indian, topped all offers with $4,500, and Thorpe came to the Polo Grounds in 1913. The Giants were loaded with talent, and McGraw did not need Thorpe. "If he hits in batting practice he'll be a big draw," said McGraw, who had no intention of using him in the lineup. On the bench the Indian sulked; he practiced half-heartedly and off the field succumbed to his weakness—firewater. Thorpe never got a chance to show what he could do as a Giant. In the few stretches when he was used regularly as an outfielder he hit well, but then McGraw would bench him for breaking training. McGraw told newspapermen that Thorpe couldn't hit a curve, which may or may not have been true. He didn't have much of a chance to show his talents. Traded to the Braves in 1919, he played sixty games and hit .327, however. This was his last year in big-league ball. He played in the minors and starred in pro football until he was forty. Then his career faded out. Despite his mediocre baseball showing, Thorpe remains the supreme athlete of all time.

Left, a fair gymnast in bloomers and sailor's blouse. Puritanism and the false modesty of the Victorian period kept the girls under wraps for generations. A strong prejudice in England and in this country against women using their muscles for anything but household tasks confined them to only a few sports in the last century, and those sports were the most refined—archery, croquet, and lawn tennis, and perhaps a little golf. If a lady engaged in gymnastic exercises she was careful to have every inch of her anatomy covered by a decorous but hardly decorative "gym suit" (left). Below, the girls, fully clothed, get off the mark on a fifty-yard dash with "hobble" skirts trailing.

In the early 1900's basketball enjoyed a wave of popularity among the college girls. The picture at the left captioned "A New Game for Women" shows a contest between students of Stanford University and visiting players from England. The contemporary commentator observes: The players are divided into two teams, each team consisting of from five to eleven players, whose object it is to knock the ball into the basket-net which represents their opponents' goal. In addition to the two-net goals, there is a third net, erected on one side of the playground. A ball in either of the net-goals counts two points to the scoring side; a ball in the neutral net counts one. The three net-bearing poles form a triangle. The umpire is placed on the centre line.

Although the picture below doesn't indicate it, one of the sports in which women are on a par with men is trapshooting. This photograph was taken in 1916, about the time when women first took up the sport in this country.

The acceptance of women in sports is due to some extent to the performances of the three female stars shown on these two pages. Above is Margaret Curtis, of Boston, who, with her sister, Harriet, was a winner of the Women's Golf Championship four times. Margaret (Little Peggy, as she was called before she filled out) won the title in 1907, '11, and '12; Harriet won it in 1906, and the next year handed the cup to her sister when the two met in the final round.

May Sutton (above, right) was America's first woman tennis player of international stature. A court prodigy, she won the Pacific Southwest Championship in 1900 at the age of thirteen, the National in 1904, and was twice winner at Wimbledon. She married Tom Bundy—National doubles champion with Red McLoughlin in 1912, '13, and '14—and helped found a California tennis dynasty.

More than any other woman, Eleanora Sears

(opposite page) blazed the trail for women in sports. A Boston society girl, Miss Sears kicked over the traces and went in for sports with masculine vigor. She played what is called "a man's game" in numerous sports and she was good at all of them. She was an excellent tennis player, a good rifle shot, a powerful swimmer, a fine golfer, and a squash player of championship caliber (National Women's Singles Champion in 1928 at the age of forty-four). Miss Sears defied convention, wore men's clothes when she felt like it, and challenged the boys to anything, especially automobile and motor-boat races. Every year she used to hike from Providence to Boston, a distance of forty-four miles. At first the daring young woman horrified New England conservatives with her tomboyish activities. But she demonstrated that a woman could play men's games like a man without causing a revolution. She won her cause, and was the prime liberator of women in sports.

CHAPTER FOUR

The Golden Age 1919—1930

America's zaniest and most colorful period of sports took place in the Tremendous Twenties. It was an age of champions, of extraordinary events and superb performances, an age of public idolatry and fabulous purses. Never before, nor since, has there been such a concentration of athletic genius in so many fields of sports.

Why did the twenties produce such an array of talent? There is no single answer, if indeed there is any explanation at all. History shows us that various fields of human endeavor from time to time reach a peak, a golden age. Generally the phenomenon is marked by good times and by the presence of gifted writers to dramatize the events and personalities of the time. The pattern fits sport's Golden Age. It arrived with prosperity, following the post-war depression, and there were brilliant chroniclers on hand to vivify it. In the press box were such facile writers and wits as W. O. McGeehan, Damon Runyon, Heywood Broun, Ring Lardner, and Westbrook Pegler, to name a few. And in the field were great performers for them to write about. This may explain in part the phenomenon of the Golden Age, but it is probably safer to say that it just happened, and no one really knows why.

Baseball, football, boxing, golf, tennis, polo, swimming, track and field, and the turf were rich with champions and near-champions, whose records still stand and whose deeds are still heralded. Youthful fans, who weren't around during the twenties, can argue that there are just as many stars today and that most of the records of the old-timers have long since been wiped from the books. True enough, many of the old marks have gone. But that is to be expected. The games have changed; the rules are different. Equipment is better. Tracks are faster, golf courses easier, and so on. The athletes of today cannot be fairly compared with those of yesterday—not by figures, at any rate. But it cannot be disputed that the great performers of the twenties stood out from their fellows to a greater extent than did those of any other period.

It is significant that when the Associated Press polled some four hundred U.S. sports writers and broadcasters in 1950 to name the greatest athletes of the present century, the champions of the twenties led in six of the nine sports polled. Only in football, basketball, and track did they fail to reach the top, but their names were high on the list in those three sports. Red Grange was right behind Jim Thorpe in football; Paavo Nurmi was topped by Jesse Owens and Jim Thorpe in track; and in basketball Nat Holman was third to George Mikan and Hank Luisetti. Now look at the other six sports, where the stars of the Golden Age swept the field: baseball—Babe Ruth; boxing—Jack Dempsey; golf—Bobby Jones; horse racing—Man O'War; swimming—Johnny Weismuller; tennis—Bill Tilden.

They were more than record-breakers, these athletes of the twenties, more than men of great skill and competitive ability. They had color, that intangible quality that put them above the great ones of every other age. Call it crowd appeal, class, or personality—whatever you will—they had it.

The Golden Age began in 1919, and it started off with a bang. That was the year that Babe Ruth, playing his last season in Boston, hit 29 homers for a new record and pitched 13 games. Jack Dempsey cut down the giant Willard to win the world heavyweight title, and Man O'War launched his career as a two-year-old.

Babe Ruth

Bobby Jones

Jack Dempsey

Bill Tilden

"Big Red," as Man O'War was called, was such a handsome, impressive-looking horse (16½ hands, 1,375 pounds) that he was an odds-on favorite in his very first start as a green two-year-old. He lived up to his looks, winning by six lengths, and from then on he was the odds-on favorite in every race he ran. Three times he went to the post a 1-to-100 choice. For two brilliant seasons (1919–1920) the big horse amazed turf followers with his speed and regal appearance. He won twenty out of twenty-one races, losing only to the aptly named Upset by a half-length because of a bad start and a bad ride. They met several times again, but Upset never could repeat his victory. In 1920

Man O'War broke either a track record or a world record in eight of his eleven starts, and he was pressed only once. If he had needed to go all-out in his races, he might have set a record every time. He won the Belmont Stakes by 20 lengths, the Lawrence Realization Stakes by 100 lengths. Only once did jockey Clarence Kummer (above) ever touch him with the bat. That was when he raced John P. Grier at Aqueduct, and the two thoroughbreds matched stride for stride until they came into the stretch. Then Kummer touched Big Red for the first time. The horse leaped into the lead with a mighty bound and won going away. Since Man O'War's day many horses have won more money, but he still stands above them in class.

Earl Sande, a wizard in the saddle, knew what kind of horse Big Red was. Johnny Loftus and Clarence Kummer had been riding him for owner Sam Riddle, but racing fans were demanding the perfect combination—the greatest horse and the greatest jockey, Man O' War and Sande. Riddle let Sande ride him in the Miller Stakes at Saratoga. It was their only meeting. Thirty years after the race, Sande said, "That day I knew I was riding the greatest horse ever bred for running." Sande should know. He rode them all, stake-winners and platers. In 3,663 starts, he was in the money over 60 per cent of the time, and his lifetime winning percentage (.26) has never been touched. One day at Havre de Grace he rode six straight winners. Sande was tops.

The leading horse in the picture below is Billy Barton, who won so many jumping races that he was known as the Man O' War of point-to-point racing. Owned by Howard Bruce of Baltimore, the horse was converted from a flat racer in the mid-twenties when he was five years old. As a steeplechaser, he bowed to none over the toughest courses in the country.

Most youngsters today are no more than vaguely aware that the man they have seen in the movies flashing through the water with pursuing crocodiles in his wake once held sixty-seven swimming records and was supreme in world competition at any distance between fifty yards and a half-mile. The man is Johnny Weissmuller. In his prime he was lean and powerful, with tremendous depth of chest and unusual buoyancy—the physical gifts that make a great swimmer. He could drive himself through the water with such force that his back was above the surface almost to the waist. Weissmuller was a product of Chicago's public pools. Bill Bachrach, swimming coach of the Illinois A.C., took the lad in hand, and launched him at the National Outdoor meet in 1921. Johnny was only sixteen then, but he won national titles at 50 and 220 yards, defeating experienced and mature competitors. Invincible in the sprints, he could go distance, as his world mark for 880 yards testifies. For good measure he hung up a couple of back-stroke records. At the time young Weissmuller first appeared, Duke Kahanamoku of Hawaii was the world's outstanding swimmer. Holder of the 100-yard record, the Duke had captured an Olympic swimming title by winning the 100 metres at Stockholm in 1912. At Antwerp eight years later he was still supreme. It was not until 1924 that the two great swimmers met in the Olympics in Paris. Weissmuller, then at his peak, was forced to make a new world record in the 100 metres to defeat the aging Duke, who was right behind him. The Chicago marvel went on to further triumphs. He was king of the waters at sixteen and remained king until his retirement in 1929.

Trudy—the world knew her by no other name after her triumph—learned to swim at the Woman's Swimming Association of New York, a little club formed by a group of business girls. A shy, brown-haired girl, she was the daughter of a German-American delicatessen owner. Trudy was a prodigy in the water. At fourteen she won an international three-mile swim in New York Bay against fifty of the best women swimmers of England and America. Soon afterward she began to lower world free-style marks from 100 to 800 meters. Grateful to the club which had given her a start, she decided one summer to try the Channel, in the hope that it would make her club famous if she succeeded. She made an attempt in 1925 and failed. But the following year, without any fanfare or publicity, she mastered the tricky rip tides and choppy waves of the Channel, crossing from France to England in the record time of 14 hours and 31 minutes. New York put on a ticker-tape celebration for her when she returned, which still remains as the wildest, most enthusiastic greeting ever given a woman. Other women have made the swim since, but Trudy showed the way.

Gertrude Ederle shared the spotlight with Johnny Weismuller in the twenties when she became the first woman in history to swim the English Channel. She is shown here about to enter the water, coated with grease to keep her warm in the Channel's frigid waters. It added several pounds to her weight.

Charley Paddock's spectacular jump finish was copied by schoolboy sprinters the country over when the California speedster was burning up the tracks in the twenties. He would take off about ten feet from the tape and lunge into it with both feet off the ground, his arms thrust upward. It was theatrical and had no value, but in the twenties youngsters were adopting the gestures and styles of their heroes in many sports. Celebrated in the nation's sports pages as the "Fastest Human," Paddock was a chunky youth with terrific leg drive and high knee action. He first won fame as a winner in the Inter-Allied Games of 1919, when he was eighteen. Rarely was he beaten when he was at his best, between 1920 and 1924. He set records in all the standard sprints from 100 to 300 yards, including "bastard" marks at such distances as 90, 110, 130, and 175 yards, which only record-hunters care about. He was the national 100-yard champion in 1921 and 1924, the national 220-yard champion in 1920, 1921, and 1924. He took part in three Olympics, but won only one race—the 100 meters in 1920. Whether he won or lost, he was always in the limelight, always the Fastest Human, with the sensational jump finish.

Paavo Nurmi was the man who raced the stop-watch. He ignored his competitors but would keep up a relentless, mechanical pace throughout a race, glancing at his stopwatch from time to time. He knew what he could do. A distance runner who had won four gold medals in the 1924 Olympics, he came to the United States from Finland in 1925. He toured the country and ran away from all opposition from the mile up, breaking world records almost every time he started. He had never run indoors before, but it made no difference. The Phantom Finn broke thirty-nine world records on his American tour, among them the mile in 4:10.4. He was the first man to better nine minutes for two miles. A long-legged, stolid fellow with a subnormal heart beat, Nurmi left more records behind, defeated more men over more distances than any other runner in history. He was the greatest distance runner ever known.

For forty years now, Clarence DeMar, a Yankee sprinter, has been running in the annual Boston Marathon, which is held every Patriot's Day (April 19). The event draws a field of more than 200 scantily clad runners and lures 500,000 spectators, who line the streets ten-deep over the long, weary route from suburban Hopkinton to Boston. A medal and a wreath of laurel go to the winner, nothing else. It's run for love and has been ever since it was started in 1897 by the Boston Athletic Association. Of all the competitors over the years, the outstanding one has been DeMar, who won so often in the twenties that he was known as De-Marathon. His first victory came in 1911 and was followed by triumphs in 1922, 1923, 1924, 1927, 1928, and 1930 —an all-time record for the race. DeMar never won any Olympic title (he ran third in 1924), but he beat the best in the world in Boston seven times.

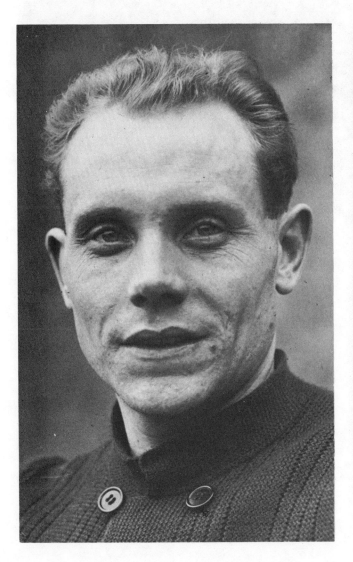

Harold (Brick) Muller was a giant redhead with huge hands who could throw a football 60 yards on a dead line. He played end on California's so-called Wonder Team of the early twenties and was the first Far West player to make All-America. As good a receiver as he was a passer, Muller was superb defensively, fast as a sprinter, and had enough spring in his legs to place second in the high jump in the 1920 Olympics—an all-around man. Brick made a play in the 1921 Rose Bowl game against Ohio State that they still talk about. Standing just beyond the midfield stripe, he uncorked a pass to Brodie Stephens, the other end, who caught it on the goal line. Brick's great performances put California on the football map. From 1920 through 1924 the Golden Bears won 44 games, tied four and lost none.

Quarterback Bo McMillin (right) and his Praying Colonels from Kentucky's tiny Centre College came up to Cambridge in 1921 to try the impossible. Harvard had whipped them, 31 to 14, the year before, and no one expected them to fare any better this time. Harvard was a mighty football power then and had not been defeated in four years. But the Centre squad of only fifteen men was bursting with talent. All-Americans McMillin and Red Roberts led the Kentuckians to a 6–0 victory. The picture below shows the Praying Colonels (they prayed in the locker room before every game) pressing Harvard on the Crimson 13-yard line. When the Colonels returned home after the victory they were wildly received throughout Kentucky. The state's governor, Edwin P. Morrow, exulted: "I'd rather be Bo McMillan right now than the governor of Kentucky."

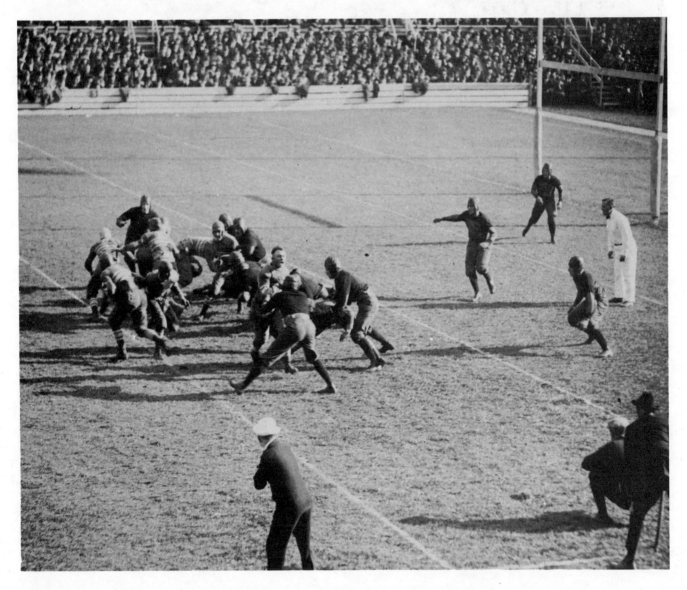

Knute K. Rockne (opposite page) was an immigrant boy from Norway who became the greatest of all football coaches. More than anyone else, he popularized the game and made Notre Dame, where he was head coach from 1918 until his death in 1931, the country's outstanding football institution. During his thirteen-year regime his teams won 105 games, lost 12, and were tied 5 times—a record no other coach can claim. A football genius with a magnetic personality, Rockne was idolized by all who knew him. Such was his impact on the game that within a few months after his death eight books about him were published.

The Four Horsemen, a catch-phrase originated by Grantland Rice in describing Rockne's 1924 backfield, was the fastest and smoothest working quartet in Notre Dame's history. Above (from left to right) they are: Jim Crowley and Don Miller, halfbacks, Elmer Layden, fullback, and Harry Stuhldreher, quarterback. Averaging only 158 pounds, the deceptive backfield functioned behind a rugged line known as the Seven Mules. The 1924 team was undefeated and untied in ten games against the country's best. Of Rockne's five unbeaten teams (1919, 1920, 1924, 1929, and 1930), this one was the most widely heralded.

Harold (Red) Grange used to lug ice during the summer months in his home town of Wheaton, Illinois, to get in shape for football. He was the game's most publicized and glamorous figure, nationally known as the Flying Terror and the Galloping Ghost. The last name stuck and is the one he's known by today. For the redhead was a ghost on the field, the most spectacular runner of any day.

He was a good punter, could pass well, and was an effective blocker, but as a broken-field runner there has never been anything like him. A 175-pound six-footer, he was fast and had a twisting, turning style as he criss-crossed the field shedding tacklers in his wake. Red played halfback for Illinois, coached by Bob Zuppke, and was named All-America in 1923, 1924, and 1925.

The Galloping Ghost had many brilliant after-noons, but his greatest single performance was against Michigan in 1924. The Wolverines had never met Grange (Illinois and Michigan did not play in 1923), but they were prepared to smear him every time he took the ball. On the kickoff Grange caught the ball on his own 5-yard line and ran 95 yards for a touchdown. He went 67, 55 and 45 yards for three more touchdowns before the game was 12 minutes old! Red was taken out then but returned in the third quarter to toss a touchdown pass and make one him-self on a 15-yard scamper around end. Illinois won, 39–14, with Grange responsible for 5 touchdowns and a stupendous gain of 402 yards on the ground. Red went on to further glory in games against Penn, Chicago, and Ohio State, and, after his last game in 1925, his jersey bearing the famous number 77 was forever retired. Red then turned pro and went on the road with the Chicago Bears, playing before packed stadiums at every appearance. He drew 72,000 people in New York in December, 1925, a record crowd for a pro game. Single-handedly he took professional football out of the doldrums and established the sport.

Britishers were thinking of Tommy Hitchcock when they said, "Polo is a Persian invention, a British sport, and an American profession." The saying, inspired by the regular drubbings they took from our international teams in the twenties and thirties—six straight defeats—was not a fair description. Hitchcock was no pro, of course, but no one was ever more devoted to the game or ever played it as well for so many years. From the time he got his ten-goal rating in 1922 (the absolute top) until the advent of World War II, he dominated the game as no other man has. He was the symbol of attack, the aggressive down-field charge with little regard for defense, but he could wield a mallet with the deft touch of a fencer when he had to. A six-footer, Hitchcock's life was as dynamic as his polo game. At sixteen he quit school to join the Lafayette Escadrille. After bagging three German planes, he was shot down and captured but escaped from a moving train and made his way to Switzerland. As commander of a Mustang fighter group in World War II, he crashed to his death in England in 1944.

Here (right) the Prince of Wales attends the 1924 matches at Meadow Brook, where Hitchcock rode supreme—as he did for twenty-three years.

Nat Holman (left) was to basketball in the Golden Age of sports what Ruth was to baseball and Grange to football. He was the first basketball player to gain nation-wide attention. A truly great passer, he threw the ball with no spin, making it easy to handle, and he could thread a needle with it. He was a dead shot, fast and elusive. In 1921 Holman joined the Original Celtics (above), a professional barnstorming team of New Yorkers, organized in 1914. The team toured the country for seven years and won twenty games for every one lost. Their complete record was 1,320 won, 66 lost. One season (1922–1923) they won 102 and lost 6. So good were they that soon after they joined the American League in the mid-twenties they were broken up and the players were distributed among other cities to give the league balance. They were too good.

The game Dr. Naismith invented in 1891 grew so fast that by the twenties there was scarcely a Y.M.C.A., college, or school in the country without a team. (The picture below, of a Princeton–West Point game in 1928, is typical of the pre-Garden era, when basketball was played on home courts.) Many are the reasons for the game's phenomenal rise, the chief one being, perhaps, that it requires no elaborate or costly equipment. Any school can afford to field a team. And, unlike football or baseball it demands no depth of manpower. Injuries are negligible, and it is more of a team game than any other. Everyone shares in handling the ball and scoring goals. There are no key positions such as the pitcher's in baseball or the quarterback's in football. Basketball today is played in some seventy-five countries and in this country attracts more participants and more spectators than any other team game.

Ice hockey, like basketball, is a newcomer to this country. The Canadian-born sport was first played at Halifax, where, in its Neanderthal days, players used a round puck (above) and strapped blades on their shoes. Long before the game crossed the border, it was an organized sport, played with skill by Canadians. Its history in this country is spotty: A student from Montreal is supposed to have introduced the game to his classmates at Johns Hopkins in 1895 and formed the first college team; it was taken up by a few New England colleges at about that time but made little progress at first because of the lack of good skaters; skating clubs in several Northern cities put teams on the ice in the '90's, and in 1896 the American Amateur Hockey League was formed. As the game spread, American players improved, but they could never compare with Canada's best.

One of the few who could was Hobey Baker (left), Princeton's hockey and football captain in 1913. Baker was head and shoulders above the college hockey players of his time, as good as any Canadian pro. He was elected in 1946 to Hockey's Hall of Fame at Kingston, Ontario, the only American amateur to be so honored.

Professional big-league hockey came here to stay in 1924 when Boston joined the National Hockey League, soon to be followed by New York, Chicago, and Detroit. The furiously fast pro game immediately caught on with American fans, even though nine out of ten players are Canadians.

Jack Dempsey electrified the boxing world when he came out of the West in 1918 and bowled over a row of heavyweights with one-round knockouts. Ring fans had never seen anything like his savage, two-handed attack. The moment the gong sounded, he seemed to burn with a white-hot rage; he'd come out with a rush, punch with both hands, and keep punching until his man went down. He was all fighter—a tough, 190-pounder with whipcord muscles and a scowling face. It was a one-sided slaughter when he met Willard at Toledo on July 4, 1919, for the title. Dempsey blasted the gigantic champion to the canvas seven times in the first round. Willard had had enough by the end of the third. His cheek bone split, his nose smashed, and his whole body a mass of red welts, Willard told his seconds to throw in the towel. It was the worst beating the champion had ever taken.

Tex Rickard was quick to see Dempsey's possibilities as a gate attraction. Even though the fighter had finessed serving in World War I and was hooted as a draft dodger, Rickard knew that fans would always pay to see a murderous puncher. They had not had much to look at since Jeffries' day. (Johnson had fled to Europe with the title, and the lumbering Willard, while champion, had fought only once in his four-year reign—in a dull, no-decision contest against Frank Moran.) Rickard looked around for an opponent for Dempsey and hit upon Georges Carpentier, a handsome, urbane Frenchman with a splendid war record. A clever boxer with a fair punch, Carpentier had stopped the fading Battling Levinsky to win the light-heavyweight crown. The Frenchman never

in his career scaled over the light-heavyweight limit and was not in Dempsey's class. But no matter. The match was a promoter's dream: a boxer against a fighter, the hero and the villain in combat. It was the perfect combination. Expertly ballyhooed by Rickard, the fight made ring history. It was the first million-dollar gate ($1,789,238), the first time a championship fight was broadcast, and had the greatest attendance of any fight to date (80,000). (Below, Dempsey slips Carpentier's left jab.) It was Dempsey all the way except for a hard right to the jaw that Carpenter landed in round two. It staggered Jack momentarily but he recovered quickly. He put Carpenter away in the fourth. It developed later that Rickard had urged Dempsey to go easy for a while.

The wildest, most frenzied action-packed battle in heavyweight history took place when Dempsey and Luis Firpo had it out like a couple of Pier-6 brawlers on the night of September 14, 1923, in New York. In three minutes and fifty-seven seconds of whirlwind milling, Firpo went down seven times in the first round, knocked Dempsey through the ropes, brought the champion to his knees in the second round, and was then flattened for keeps. Above is Dempsey going out of the ring (from a lithograph by George Bellows). It was a foul fight all the way. Almost every time Dempsey knocked Firpo down he stood right over him and clubbed him to the canvas as Luis tried to regain his feet.

"All the News That's Fit to Print."

The New York Times.

THE WEATHER
Showers today and tonight, followed by clearing and cooler tomorrow.
Temperatures yesterday—Max. 69, Min. 62.

VOL. LXXVI....No. 25,080. ....   NEW YORK, FRIDAY, SEPTEMBER 24, 1926.   TWO CENTS in Greater New York | THREE CENTS Within 200 Miles | FOUR CENTS Elsewhere in the U. S.

TUNNEY WINS CHAMPIONSHIP, BEATS DEMPSEY IN 10 ROUNDS; OUTFIGHTS RIVAL ALL THE WAY, DECISION NEVER IN DOUBT; 135,000 PAY MORE THAN $2,000,000 TO SEE BOUT IN THE RAIN

After the Firpo brawl, Dempsey was thought to be invincible and, when he agreed to meet Gene Tunney for the title, only one or two boxing writers believed the challenger had a chance. In Tunney's mind there never had been any doubt. A cool, intelligent boxer with unlimited determination, Tunney was not an exciting performer, but he always won. He knew that Dempsey could massacre big, slow-moving men like Willard and Firpo but was not so effective against a good defensive boxer. Tunney accordingly planned to keep on the move, counter and jab, and outbox his man. That was the story of the fight. Dempsey, who hadn't laced on a glove for three years, was unable to land a solid punch in ten rounds. At the end, when Tunney's hand was raised, Dempsey's face was unrecognizable.

Tunney was never as popular as Dempsey. In many ways he was like Corbett: he had deposed an idol, he was essentially a ring scientist, and he was reserved in manner. After Dempsey lost his crown at Philadelphia, the ex-champion took on Jack Sharkey, an in-and-outer from Boston. The bout was held to determine a challenger for Tunney's title. Dempsey, now thirty-two, was taking a fine lacing until the seventh round, when he hit Sharkey below the belt, then knocked him out with a left hook to the jaw as the Bostonian dropped his arms to appeal to the referee. The outcome created some controversy, but it was a popular victory. Dempsey could do no wrong. He had earned the right to meet Tunney and try to do what no heavyweight champion had yet done—regain his title. The second Dempsey–Tunney fight was held in Soldiers' Field, Chicago, on September 22, 1927—a year, less one day, after the Philadelphia fight. More than 100,000 people were on hand, and most of them hoped that Dempsey would stiffen the champion. For six rounds it was a replica of their first fight. Tunney stabbed his man continuously, outboxed him, and was never in danger. Then, in the seventh, it happened: Dempsey caught Tunney in a corner and nailed him with a series of lefts and rights to the jaw. Down went Tunney, dazed and battered. Referee Dave Barry quickly ordered Dempsey to a neutral corner, but the ex-champion refused to move. Before the fight the Illinois Boxing Commission had conferred with the fighters, and among the points brought up was the Commission's rule on a knockdown: the man scoring it must immediately go to the farthest neutral corner. If he refused, the count would not begin until he had gone. Dempsey knew this, but he did not move. When he finally did, Barry started his count at one, which gave Tunney four or five extra seconds. He got up at nine, and Dempsey flew toward him. But Tunney back-pedaled and circled out of range until his head cleared. He recovered completely in the next round and won going away. Dempsey men still say the fight should have been his, but Tunney adherents maintain that Dempsey did not obey the rules and deserved to lose. Furthermore, they say, in the twenty rounds the men fought in their two battles, Tunney won nineteen. He also won $990,000 at Chicago for thirty minutes' work—the highest pay an athlete ever got for a single performance.

The light heavyweight class had its Golden Age in the twenties when a number of first-rate men appeared and fought each other with frequency, creating much interest in the class. Among them were Tommy Loughran, Jimmy Slattery, and (right) the two bitter rivals, Jack Delaney and Paul Berlenbach (on the scales). Delaney, a handsome French-Canadian, born Ovila Chapdelaine, fought Berlenbach four times and won all but one bout.

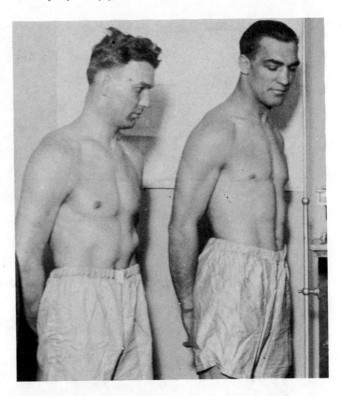

Below is Battling Siki, a Senegalese, who took Carpentier's title away from him in a bout that was supposedly fixed for the Frenchman to win. Siki lost his crown the next time out to Mike McTigue, an Irishman (below, right), in Dublin on St. Patrick's day, 1923.

This is how Babe Ruth looked when he came up from Providence in 1914 to pitch for the Red Sox. The nineteen-year-old southpaw had a blazing fast ball with nothing on it, but it was good enough to win 87 games for the Sox in the six years (1914–1919) he played there, doubling as a pitcher and outfielder. The lean, broad-shouldered youngster was a sensation from the start. He was a double star—a superb pitcher and a graceful outfielder, with tremendous power at the plate.

The Babe came at a time when he was needed most. In 1920, his first season as a Yankee, a scandal rocked the baseball world when it was revealed that eight White Sox players had sold out to gamblers and had thrown the 1919 World Series. At no time had the national pastime been in such peril as when the news broke a year after the deed. The bomb exploded just as Ruth was finishing the season with an unbelievable 54-home-run record and a batting average of .376. The next year he did even better—59 homers and a .378 average. Fans flocked to see him, attendance records were broken, and faith in the game was restored. Ruth did not do it all, of course, but the Big Fellow helped. So did the appointment of Judge Kenesaw Mountain Landis (below, left, with Yankee owner, Jacob Ruppert) as Baseball Commissioner. Before Landis' appointment, the game had been run by the National Baseball Commission, a three-man group of baseball officials. Club owners knew that if the game's prestige was ever to be restored they would have to put a non-baseball man in office and submit to his authority. The Judge was given absolute power to rule the game, and he ruled it with an iron hand until his death in 1944.

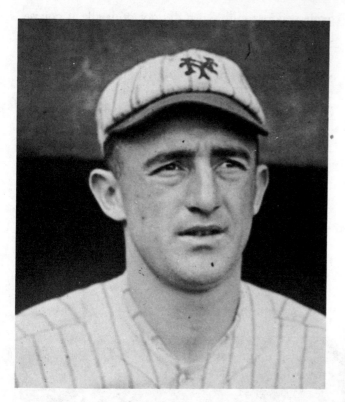

The Little Napoleon is shown below with owner Charles A. Stoneham, at the Giants–Yankee World Series in 1921. At that time, the Yankees, having no ball park of their own, shared the Polo Grounds with the Giants. This nettled the fiery McGraw, who was a firm National Leaguer all his life and hated Ban Johnson and the other league in general. (Although the first World Series was played in 1903, McGraw in 1904 refused to pit his pennant-winning Giants against the Red Sox, champions of the American League, in a post-season series. He relented in 1905, however.) The 1921 World Series to McGraw was more than a test of two teams; it was one league against the other, the old school of inside baseball against Babe Ruth, for whom McGraw had outspoken contempt. It was also a battle for the patronage of New York fans.

Before Ruth came to New York, the Yankees had never won a pennant. The Giants were the traditional New York team, the Giants of John McGraw, who had brought six flags to the Polo Grounds while the Yankees wallowed in the second division year after year.

The Giants had all the talent. Names like Christy Mathewson, Art Devlin, Iron Man Joe McGinnity, and Roger Bresnahan had brightened the rosters since the Little Napoleon first managed the club in 1902. His teams were all of the same mold—scrappy, colorful, and brainy in the McGraw tradition. One of the manager's great discoveries was Frank Frisch (above), who came from Fordham in 1919 with his diploma in his hand to don a Giant uniform. A switch hitter who could powder the ball from either side of the plate. Frisch could and did play every infield position until he finally settled down as second base. As a play maker, base runner, and hitter, the Fordham Flash earned his place in the Hall of Fame alongside of such great second basemen as Larry Lajoie, Eddie Collins, Johnny Evers, Rogers Hornsby, and Charlie Gehringer. When Frisch came to the Giants and Ruth to the Yankees, both New York teams soon climbed to the summit in their respective leagues to give the city its first Subway Series.

Great was McGraw's chagrin when the Giants dropped the first two games by shutouts to the Yankees in the 1921 Subway Series. No club had ever won a Series after losing the first two games. But better days were ahead for the McGrawmen. They took the next two, dropped one, and then went on to take the Series, 5 games to 3. (This was the last year a five-out-of-nine-game Series was played.) If McGraw's victory was sweet, it was far sweeter the following year, when the Giants white-washed their rivals without losing a game and held Ruth to two hits in seventeen times at bat for a humiliating average of .118. McGraw and the Giants were on top of the world. This was the last year the Yankees shared the Polo Grounds with the Giants, and, when the two New York clubs met for the

third straight time in 1923, the big Bronx Stadium was jammed with a record crowd of 55,307.

The Yankees lost the first game and by so doing established a record of having lost eight straight World Series games—the last three in 1921, all four the next year, and the 1923 opener. But Ruth, who had had a great year, hitting .393 for the highest average of his career, made up for his miserable showing in the previous Series by poling out three homers and averaging .368. The Yankees won, 4 games to 2. It was their first world championship. The Giant regime was coming to an end. The Yankees were on the upswing, about to establish the most powerful and enduring dynasty in baseball history. (Below, a typical World Series scene in the massive, three-tier Yankee Stadium.)

A young athlete from Columbia University named Henry Louis Gehrig appeared in the Yankee lineup at first base in a few games in 1923 and then was shipped to Hartford by manager Miller Huggins. The big, amiable New Yorker (he stood six feet one and weighed 210) was ungainly around the bag at first, but he never stopped trying to improve himself. In spring training he was always the first man on the field and the last one off. Lou's perseverance paid off. He became a smooth-working fielder and a terrific slugger. After burning up the International League in 1924 by hitting .369, he was brought back to New York. On June 1, 1925, Lou took over first base from Wally Pipp and from that day on didn't miss a game for fourteen years. Not once was he out of the lineup in 2,130 games, a consecutive mark that no one will ever catch. The iron-bodied Gehrig was one of the game's great hitters. He batted .295 his first year and was never below .300 for the next twelve. It was Ruth and Gehrig, the Home-Run King and the Crown Prince, who struck terror in pitchers for the next several years. Never before or since have there been two such power-hitters on the same team. Lou followed the Babe at bat. With Gehrig coming up, the pitcher couldn't afford to walk Ruth; he had to get the ball over. Thus Lou was responsible in some measure for Ruth's success. Lou was over-shadowed by Ruth and later, after the Babe was through, by Joe DiMaggio. He didn't mind as long as his team won—and it generally did.

The Babe was at his zenith in 1927 when he slammed 60 homers. (On the right he reaches the top of his career by hitting homer number 60 off Tom Zachary of Washington in the Yankee Stadium on September 30, 1927). That was the year of years for the Yankees. They were out of sight in October, finishing 19 games ahead of the second place A's. The 1927 team was the mightiest of all the Yankee teams. They had terrific power at the plate, were superb defensively and had a crack pitching staff. In the "perfect outfield" of Ruth, Bob Meusel and Earle Combs, Meusel with .337 was the lightest hitter. The team was unstoppable and when they faced the Pirates in the Series there was no question about who would win. The Yankees blew them apart in four straight games.

Year after year Yankee fans were treated to the familiar sight shown below. The Bam would get up, hit one out of the park, and trot around the bases on his spindly legs to get Gehrig's handshake at the plate.

"Don't wake me up, let me dream," murmured Uncle Robbie in the dugout one day as he watched three Dodger base runners arrive simultaneously on third base and stand there. Uncle Wilbert Robinson (above), manager of the Dodgers in the mid-twenties, when they were at their daffiest, was used to such things. The light-hearted Daffiness Boys were the delight of baseball scribes, but not of Dodger fans. The players disregarded all the known rules of baseball and of common sense. They batted out of turn, stole bases with the sacks loaded and passed each other on the base paths. And the outfielders got crowned with fly balls. Robbie's boys played out of position, ignored signals, and read newspapers in the dugout while the game was on. There was nothing the Daffiness Boys didn't do when Robbie was the pilot.

The greatest right-hand hitter who ever lived was Rogers Hornsby. He played on four National League teams and turned in the highest batting average in the history of three of them. The Rajah is the all-time batting champion of the Cards, the Braves, and the Cubs. Only during his one-year stop with the Giants (1927) was he below the club's best mark—Bill Terry's .401, made three years later. Hornsby piloted the Cards of 1926 to a World Series victory over the Yankees. He led the National League in batting for seven years, six of them in succession, and his lifetime mark is a robust .358. Three times he went over .400, once (in 1924) hitting .424 for the highest average in modern times. The big Texan was an accomplished second baseman (he led the league twice in fielding), but hitting was his specialty.

It looked as if the Yankees were going to own the American League forever when they won another flag in 1928—their sixth in eight years. But down in Philadelphia, Connie Mack had been building up a team that was about to halt the seemingly invincible New Yorkers. Mack had a ton of TNT in his line-up, with Al Simmons, Mule Haas, Bing Miller, Jimmy Foxx, and Mickey Cochrane, all good for better than .300, and a top-notch hurling staff in Lefty Grove, Rube Walberg, and George Earnshaw.

Below are the two standouts who helped bring an end to Philadelphia's fourteen-year pennant drought: Jimmy Foxx and Mickey Cochrane.

Foxx was a home-run hitter second only to Ruth and an all-around player. He was Mack's first base-man but he could—and did, before his career was over—play every position except second base in championship games. The powerfully built Marylander led the league in homers four times and came close to Ruth's best mark with 58 one year. Jimmy was a good man in every department.

There have been only one or two catchers who could be mentioned in the same breath with Mickey Cochrane. The black-haired Irishman was a flaming competitor, a fine hitter, and agile as a shortstop. For a catcher, he had unusual speed on the bases. He never batted down at the end of the line-up as most backstops do. Mickey was second or third in the batting order, even lead-off man at times.

The power-laden Athletics sent the Yankees reeling in 1929, when they won the pennant by eighteen games. They stayed on top for three years and were twice world champions. After the Athletics' three-year reign, the Yankees bounced right back again, more formidable than ever. Connie Mack never brought another pennant to Philadelphia.

In all the years since Major Walter Wingfield brought out his patented game of lawn tennis in 1873, the world has never seen anything to equal William T. Tilden, II (opposite page), the master of them all. In an age that produced Dempsey, Grange, Ruth, Weismuller, Hitchcock, and Jones, the lanky Philadelphian stood supreme. Tilden was more than a monarch; he was an artist and an actor with a strong dash of ham. He was both detested and idolized. But there was nothing on the court that he couldn't do superlatively.

Below, Tilden and Bill Johnston (in the far court) meet on the center court at Forest Hills in the finals of the 1925 National Singles Championship. The Tilden–Johnston feud, stretching over eight years, produced the most dramatic and bitterly fought tennis matches ever seen. Six times Big Bill and Little Bill clashed in the finals at Forest Hills and countless times in other tournaments. Tilden almost always won, but not before he had been given a furious battle by the pint-sized Californian.

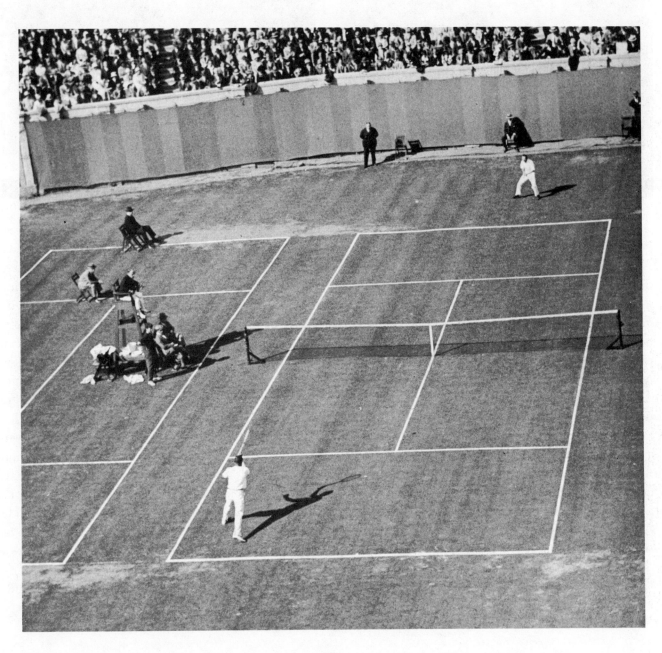

Little Bill Johnston weighed less than 125 pounds during most of his life and stood five feet, eight inches. But he made up for his slight physique with great fighting spirit. At the net he was second to none. He could call the score against any other player in the world but Tilden. The two rivals were not enemies off the court. On one occasion when Tilden, after dropping the first two sets, wore him down and came on to win the championship, he said to Little Bill, as they shook hands at the net, "You're a better player than I am, Bill. I'm just a little stronger." It was a gracious speech, but it wasn't so—not after 1919, at any rate, which was the last year that Johnston beat his rival for the national title. After that they met five times in the finals and Tilden won them all. Johnston was never disgraced in any of the matches—they were almost always close, long-drawn-out struggles—but Little Bill could never quite make it again.

No one has ever dominated a game as completely as Big Bill dominated tennis in the Golden Twenties. For ten straight years, he ranked at the top and won seven national championships, of which six (1920–1925) came consecutively. He was the first American to win the men's singles at Wimbledon, the classic crown to all tennis players. He sought it five times and won it three times (1920, 1921, and 1930). He was on eleven Davis Cup teams (a record) and led the fight that kept the Cup in this country for seven straight years. In all, he won seventy American and International titles. Tilden had the perfect tennis build and a tactical brain. He had a heavyweight's shoulders on a light frame and long springy legs. He could cover the court in three strides and was as graceful as a ballet dancer. He had everything—a cannonball serve and a paralyzing forehand and backhand. If he had any weakness, it was his tendency to let down and then stage a great recovery for the gallery.

This is the Davis Cup team of 1926, the last year of our seven-year possession of the trophy. From left to right: Big Bill, R. Norris Williams, Vincent Richards, and Little Bill Johnston. From 1920 to 1926, the United States defended the trophy against Australia, Japan, and France. Tilden began to slip a little after 1925 and as he went so went the Cup. Henri Cochet (right) brought him down in the quarter-finals of the National Championship in 1926, and in the next year Lacoste beat him in the finals. Tilden insisted that the tennis the French were playing was beyond his own game. He refused to admit that age had caught up with him (he was 34 in 1927) and that his own game was slipping. When the French took the Cup home in 1927, the United States did not see it again for ten years.

There was no love lost between these two when they met at Forest Hills on August 17, 1921. Mrs. Molla Mallory (left), who came to America from Norway, was then the country's top woman player, five times national champion. Suzanne Lenglen, the reigning queen of Wimbledon, had slighted her in the British tournament, and now, in the first meeting of the two on this side, Mrs. Mallory yearned for revenge. A few minutes after this picture was taken, the smiling Mrs. Mallory became a tigress on the court. She pummelled the French girl, 6 to 2, in the opening set—which was also the closing one. Coughing and weeping, Mlle. Lenglen staggered off the court. She had had enough.

On the opposite page is Helen Wills, of California, who ended Mrs. Mallory's reign in 1923, when, at the age of seventeen, she won her first national championship. An expressionless, placid girl, she was dubbed "Little Miss Poker Face" by sports writers. But she could hit a ball harder than any woman who ever played. Her ground strokes were so powerful and steady that she had no need to come up to the net, and rarely did. Her game was monotonous to watch, in the opinion of many tennis fans, but it was effective enough to bring her seven American titles and eight Wimbledon crowns in fifteen years—a record unmatched by any other woman.

The pictures on these two pages show Willie Hoppe, the most durable champion in sports history, in the various stages of his career. Above, the Boy Wonder, as he looked in 1906 when he went to Paris and defeated Maurice Vignaux for the world 18.1 balk-line championship. Willie was eighteen years old then, but he had been playing since he was a toddler of six, when he had to stand on a box in order to reach the table.

Both balk-line and three-cushion billiards are played on pocketless tables. In balk-line parallel lines are drawn either fourteen or eighteen inches from each cushion. The cue ball must make a carom with two object balls, but varying restrictions are made as to hitting balls in the corners or side areas of the table.

In three-cushion billiards the cue ball must hit the cushions three times before making a carom.

Here, the Boy Wonder grows older. This picture was taken in 1927, when Willie, at forty, was in the middle of his career and holder of two balk-line championships. Now and then one of his titles would be lifted by his great rival, Jake Schaefer, Jr., but there were few years when he did not hold at least one of his crowns. During his forty-seven-year career he won fifty-one world championship titles.

This is the old master in 1951, when he captured his fifth consecutive three-cushion championship. He made it six straight in 1952, then retired from competition. He was then in his sixties but he was still able to vanquish players who weren't even born when he started his extraordinary career. After his retirement, the Last Master, as he was called, gave exhibitions until his death in 1959.

This picture shows Bobby Jones a moment after he had holed out to win the British Open at Hoylake with a score of 291, halfway home in his quest of the Grand Slam. He had won the British Amateur in May, 1930, and now, a month later, with the British Open under his belt, he had two more to go—the U.S. Open and Amateur. Robert T. Jones, Jr., ("Bob" to his friends and "Bobby" in the press) began playing in tournaments at Atlanta, Georgia, when he was nine. At fourteen he was playing in major competition. It took him seven years to reach the top. Golf fans who remember Jones for his incredible feats in the latter part of his career are prone to forget that from 1916 through 1922 he played in eleven major, or national, golf championships without winning one. Once he reached the summit, however, by winning the U.S. Open in 1923, there was no stopping him. In the next stretch, which his biographer O. B. Keeler calls "the eight fat years" (1923–1930), he won thirteen national championships. "And," adds Keeler, "I'll let you in on this much: it will never happen again."

America's best woman golfer in the twenties was Glenna Collett, "the female Bobby Jones." Always a popular favorite, she won six U.S. National Amateur championships, which is more than any other golfer, man or woman, has ever won. In less than twenty years she won forty-nine major tournaments.

When a national golf Hall of Fame was proposed in the early 1950's, the first four names suggested were those of Bobby Jones, Francis Ouimet, Walter Hagen (left), and Gene Sarazen (below). They formed the base of the Hall. Sarazen, born Saracini, started as a caddy at the Apawamis Golf Club in Harrison, New York, and became a pro while still in his teens. When he was twenty-one and still an unknown kid, he astounded the golf world by winning the Open at Skokie under the noses of Hagen and Jones. To prove that he was no flash in the pan, he won the P.G.A. that year and then defeated Hagen 3 and 2 in a special 72-hole match. The cocky youngster was on top of the world, but not for long. After his second P.G.A. victory (1923), his game soured, and he went into partial eclipse for nine years, which should have been his best years. Not until 1932 did he come back, and a sensational comeback it was. That year he won both the British and U.S. Opens. The courageous little ex-caddie was on top of the world again.

On the opposite page is Walter Hagen, taking a sip out of one of the innumerable cups he won during his thirty-year career. A rollicking fellow, Sir Walter used to kid about himself when his game began to fade in the early thirties. His decline started when he started getting bad Scotch, he said. Not many experts would claim that Hagen was the greatest golfer, but most would agree that he was the fiercest competitor and the greatest match-play performer. At man-to-man battling, he outclassed them all. In 1926 he met Bobby Jones in Florida for the unofficial world championship in a match played in two installments of 36 holes each on two different courses. Jones got the beating of his life, 12 and 11. Bobby got revenge twice that season—in the U.S. and British Open championships—but the match-play licking still smarted. Sir Walter's record is nearest to that of Jones, rated on the U.S. and British Opens and the P.G.A. He won eleven major titles in all— two U.S. Opens, four British Opens, and the P.G.A. an unprecedented five times. Hagen was never ruffled by a bad shot, and he made many. He abhorred long hours of practice. "Why waste good shots in practice when you might need them in a match?" he used to say. The Haig was the most colorful golfer who ever swung a club.

When Bobby Jones came home in 1926 with the British Open in his pocket, he got the full ticker-tape treatment from elated New Yorkers and a reception at City Hall by Mayor Jimmy Walker. Bobby hadn't seen anything yet. Four years later, the year of the Grand Slam, New York put on a show that made the other seem like a dirge. A million people turned out to greet the winner of the British Open and Amateur. A trainload of Atlanta fans rolled into the city, many of whom went on to Minneapolis to watch him try for the U.S. Open at Interlachen Country Club.

It was Jones again at Interlachen in the U.S. Open. Horton Smith was two strokes ahead at the end of two rounds. But Bobby broke loose the next morning with a 68 and finished with a 287 total to win by two strokes. At that moment he became the first golfer in history to win three major championships in one year. One more, the Amateur, would make it perfect. While the country held its breath, Bobby knocked off the first four players he faced and then met Eugene Homans in the final. (Below, the eighteenth green at the Merion Cricket Club, where the Amateur was held in September, 1930. Jones, kneeling, watches Homans putt.) That night, with the fourth cup in his possession, Bobby stood on the absolute pinnacle of golfdom. Over a period of eight years he had won our National Amateur five times, our Open four times, the British Open three times, and the British Amateur once. There has never been a championship golfer in his class or one so worshipped. In the glorious Golden Age, Jones stood alone as the finest sportsman, the model of the American athlete.

CHAPTER FIVE

Sports For Everybody 1931–1952

The retirement of Bobby Jones in 1930 brought an end to the Golden Age but it by no means lessened America's interest in sports. Another batch of great performers was on the way to replace the golden boys. They were not to come all at once and crowd the stage nor would they, with one or two exceptions, dominate their various sports as had the Titans of the Twenties. Nor would they have the color or the crowd appeal of the others. But the new champions, strung out over two decades with a major depression and a world war intervening, would equal and better the performances of the old as far as the record books go. And, as is always the case in the ever changing sports scene, fans would draw comparisons between the old and the new.

Could Louis have stood up against Dempsey's two-handed relentless attack? How would the betting be on Man O' War and Citation at level weights with Sande and Arcaro in the irons? How would Jones and Hagen do in a series of matches against Nelson and Hogan? Who would you rather have playing in your backfield—the Four Horsemen or Blanchard, Davis and Tucker, Army's explosive trio? And what about the mile of the century—Nurmi and Cunningham? Unanswerable, of course, but the arguments never cease.

There is little argument, however, about America's world leadership in sport. For no other nation has ever produced so many champions or so many winning international teams. And in no other country do so many millions engage in sports or attend sporting events, or pay such a huge annual sports bill (about four billion dollars).

There have been significant changes since the twenties. First, the tempo of sports has speeded up to a point where many of the old games are hardly recognizable. More and more American fans demand more action and the scoring punch—the 35–21 football game rather than the one touchdown battle, and bigger scores in basketball, baseball and hockey.

Secondly, more people in this country are actually participating in sports, thanks in great measure to the work of the National Recreation Association. Almost unnoticed by fans whose gaze is on the headliners, this organization has revolutionized the lives of American youngsters by providing thousands of athletic fields, tennis courts, baseball diamonds and swimming pools, and furnishing equipment for the games and competent leaders to supervise them. It may seem a far cry from the neighborhood playground and gym to the World Series or the Davis Cup but in bringing sports to everybody the Association is serving as an incubator for future champions as well as bringing health and strength to millions of Americans of all ages. Sports for everybody from the playground up has been America's theme since the twenties.

The crowd likes a winner, but, when a man can lose with courage and grace, he is often admired even more than the winner. Such a man was Sir Thomas Lipton (right), a foreigner and a chronic loser, yet he had millions of Americans rooting for him whenever he came to this country to compete for "The America's Cup." Five different times, with five successive *Shamrocks*, over a period of thirty-two years (1899–1930), Sir Thomas tried to gain the Cup in American waters, and each time he failed. He wanted desperately to win it, but he never gave himself an alibi, never blamed his luck or used sharp practices. He knew how to lose. After his 1930 failure, Will Rogers suggested that everybody send a dollar apiece to buy a loving cup for Sir Thomas, bigger than the one he would have got if he had won. When the trophy was presented, the comedian said: "To possibly the world's worst yacht builder but absolutely the world's most cheerful loser."

Below is Harold S. Vanderbilt at the wheel of the *Ranger* in a practice run off Newport in 1937. Vanderbilt defended the Cup in 1930, '34, and '37, the last two times against T. O. M. Sopwith, of England.

The cup which was originally won from the British by the yacht *America* in 1851 now reposes at the New York Yacht Club, where it is bolted to a table, guarded like the Holy Grail. The specially designed wrench required to loosen the bolt is kept in the Yacht Club's safe. The cup is of silver and if melted down into bullion would probably bring less than $100. Yet it is the most expensive of all trophies because of the millions of dollars and pounds sterling that have gone into efforts to obtain or defend it. Sixteen times between 1870 and 1937 British yachts tried unsuccessfully to lift the old mug.

One of the closest calls came in 1934, when Sopwith arrived with his *Endeavour* to race against Vanderbilt's *Rainbow*. (Above, the crew of the *Endeavour* hoists the mainsail before a trial spin off Newport.) Skippered by Sopwith, the *Endeavour* won the first two races in the four-out-of-seven series, and it looked as though the wrench at the New York Yacht Club might have to be used. But Vanderbilt took the next four races, and the cup was safe. Following the fourth heat, Sopwith criticised Vanderbilt's tactics and filed a protest, but the Racing Committee denied the Englishman's claim.

Many thought that when Sopwith sailed home he would never challenge again because of the ill feeling that arose out of the controversial fourth race. But he came back three years later with the *Endeavour II*, which he had built at a cost of a million dollars. Vanderbilt's equally expensive yacht was named the *Ranger*.

Below, the yachts come to close quarters, the blue-hulled *Endeavour* on the left. There was no question about it this time. Vanderbilt won four straight races and in one established a new record over the thirty-mile course. Again Sopwith went home empty-handed. The America's Cup was not challenged again until 1958.

Gene Venzke was the first of a cluster of great milers who came together in the thirties and made track fans forget about Nurmi. Gene started off the era by winning the mile in the 1932 Millrose Games in 4:11.2, thereby smashing Joie Ray's and Nurmi's world indoor mark of 4:12, made seven years before.

Ten days later he astounded the track world with a 4:10 on the same boards. He seemed unbeatable, but he was never to reach those heights again. As long as he ran he was a great competitor and a big draw, but on the horizon were two still greater milers—Bill Bonthron and Glenn Cunningham.

Here are the three speed-milers in the Princeton Invitation Meet, June 16, 1934: Cunningham, Bonthron, and Venzke, in that order, as they finished the first lap. Bonthron, a Princeton senior, was making his last start as an undergraduate. Venzke by this time had become Cunningham's "bridesmaid" with his second-place finishes and several thirds in the furious Cunningham–Bonthron–Venzke races that had thrilled indoor track fans the previous winter. The 25,000 people in the stadium expected another close finish between Cunningham and Bonthron, but the former opened up at the half and put on such a withering finish that the Princetonian trailed by forty yards. Venzke was out of sight. The clockers blinked when they read Glenn's time—4:06.7. Two weeks later the three met again in the 1,500 meters at the National A.A.U. Championships at Milwaukee. This time it was Bonthron who put on a blazing finish to nose out Cunningham in 3:48.8, a world record. Venzke was, as usual, the bridesmaid, finishing third. The magnificent Cunningham–Bonthron duels of the mid-thirties stimulated interest in track the country over. Whenever the two met, it was a standing-room-only affair. First one would win and then the other and, unlike the Princeton race, they would usually be glued together at the tape. After Bonthron gave up running, Cunningham went on to become the outstanding miler of his time.

These two pictures show Bill Bonthron and Glenn Cunningham as they looked when they were burning up the tracks. Glenn's unorthodox running—turning in a faster second half than his first—brought him more medals than any other American miler. For seven years he was never out of training. In that span he ran the mile more than twenty times under 4:10, more often than all his rivals combined.

On the opposite page, some of the crack milers of Cunningham's time. Top, left, is Jack Lovelock, of New Zealand, mile record-holder in 1933; on the right is Archie San Romani, who defeated Cunningham and Don Lash at Princeton in 1937; lower left, Chuck Fenske, conqueror of Cunningham in 1939, when Glenn was beginning to slow up; far right, Gil Dodds, whose career began as Cunningham's was ending. Dodds and Leslie MacMitchell took over the mile after Cunningham retired.

The greatest day any track athlete ever had was the epic day when Jesse Owens (shown above breaking the tape in the 220-yard low hurdles) shattered five world records and tied a sixth in the Big Ten meet at Ann Arbor, Michigan. Here is what Owens did on that memorable afternoon of May 25, 1935: he ran the 100-yard dash in 9.4 to tie the world mark of Frank Wykoff; he won the 220 in 20.3 to better the previous time of Roland Locke by three tenths of a second; he sped over the 220-yard low hurdles in 22.6 to take four tenths of a second off the mark set by Normal Paul; he broad-jumped 26 feet, 8¼ inches to beat the mark of Chuhei Nambu of Japan by 6⅛ inches. While he was making new world marks in the 220 and the 220 low-hurdles, he also made official

records in the 200-meter distance for both events. In one afternoon, the Ohio State Negro wiped the names of five world-record holders off the books. The marks he shattered represented the best efforts of athletes from various parts of this country and abroad and covered a period of several years. They all went by the boards in a couple of hours, and one man did it all. That afternoon Owens was the perfect racing machine, a human bullet. He did more than shave the records; he lowered them in such decisive fashion that three of his marks were still standing fifteen years later. His broad jump mark, the last to go, remained on the books for twenty-five years. Surely, no one will ever have such a day as Jesse had when he made those records.

Track coaches have a saying: "Sprinters, like poets, are born, not made." Jesse Owens was born a sprinter. (He was also, incidentally, born James Cleveland Owens. The "Jesse" came from "J. C.") Trying to fathom the reason for Owens' remarkable speed, Lawson Robertson, mentor of U.S. Olympic track teams for years, once said, "Nervous energy makes for great speed and explosive energy. The average Negro track athlete is built for speed. The legs are symmetrical, the muscles seldom bunch. Owens has the finest pair of legs I have ever seen. They are not ideal for sustained effort and would probably not stand up well on a football field. But for speed and explosive effort, Owens' legs are perfect." The perfect legs (note, below) carried him to further triumphs in the 1936 Olympics, when he won the 100 and 200 meters and the broad jump and was lead-off man on the winning 400-meter relay team.

Here, Jesse Owens stands on the victory pedestal after winning the broad jump with a new Olympic record of 26 feet, 5⁵⁄₁₆ inches. Behind him is second-place Luz Long of Germany; in front, Naoto Tajima of Japan, who took third place. The fable persists that Hitler refused to shake hands with Owens. The facts are that Hitler greeted the German and Finnish winners on the first day of the games (August 1, 1936) and left the stadium before Cornelius Johnson, American Negro, won the high jump. On the advice of Olympic officials, Hitler greeted no more champions at any time during the rest of the games. Owens did not compete until the third day. If anyone was slighted it was Johnson, not Owens—which is not important, perhaps. What is important is that the name of Jesse Owens is hammered deep in bronze in the Berlin stadium, and it appears there four times, more often than Hitler's name ever did.

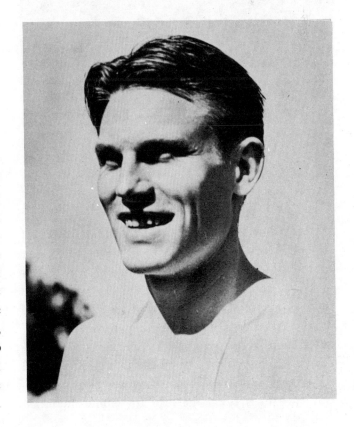

The first man in history to clear fifteen feet in the pole vault was Cornelius (Dutch) Warmerdam (above, and right), who broke through the ceiling in 1940 with a 15-foot, 1⅛-inch vault. The most difficult as well as the most spectacular event in track and field athletics, the pole vault requires the speed of a sprinter, split-second timing, and the agility of an acrobat. Warmerdam, a California high school teacher, climbed up inch by inch until he got to the summit in 1943 with a 15-foot, 8½-inch vault. He was then twenty-seven-years old. He retired in 1944, having broken through 15 feet forty-three times. No one has ever had such flawless form. Vaulters took twenty-two years to reach 16 feet; then came the fiber-glass pole and they topped 17 feet quickly.

"Snowshoe" Thomson, one of the pioneers of American skiing, in all probability never had a pair of snowshoes on in his life. Thomson was master of the wooden wings, which in his day were called snowshoes, not skis. The webbed footgear invented by the American Indian was known as "the pads" in the high Sierras along the California-Nevada border, where Snowshoe carried the United States mail for twenty years. Thomson, who was born in Norway, began carrying the mail to remote mountain settlements soon after the 1849 California gold rush. Negotiating a ninety-one mile route, (Placerville, California, to Carson City, Nevada, and return) with a pack of about 100 pounds, he had to cross mountains and go through appalling snow drifts, often in sub-zero weather. He never failed to make it. His feats of endurance and courage are still remembered in the Sierra country, where he is revered as 'the greatest snowshoer of them all."

The "snowshoers" of Thomson's day, as the pictures on this page point out, used a single stout pole and skis of ten to twelve feet in length. Thomson's prowess on the boards interested the miners of the Sierras, who were idle by winter, and they took up skiing for fun. As early as 1850, tournaments were held, and in 1867 the Alturas Snowshoe Club, of La Porte, California, was formed. It was the world's first ski club, pre-dating Norway's Christiania Ski-klub (Europe's first) by ten years. The sport may have been hundreds of years old in the Scandinavian countries, but the American miners were the first to organize it and form a club. The Father of American skiing was a bearded Yankee from Skowhegan, Maine, named Isaac Steward, who founded the Alturas Club. He was also a good man on the boards. Steward held all the downhill and obstacle records in the '70's, by which time hundreds of miners were competing in ski tournaments.

Above, the start; below, the flyers pose to show the downhill racing style. These pictures were taken in the '80's, when skiing was a full-fledged sport in California and Nevada.

Until 1930, skiing in the East was confined to a handful of Scandinavians and to small groups such as the Dartmouth Outing Club in Hanover, New Hampshire, which was formed in 1910. The next year, due to the energy of Fred T. Harris (Dartmouth, '11), the Dartmouth Winter Carnival was started. It attracted a few outdoor enthusiasts to Hanover every year. But the sport grew slowly. For years, anyone who appeared in a train or on the streets with a pair of skis over his shoulders was likely to find a crowd of small boys jeering at his heels and was regarded as a harmless eccentric by adults. A few hardy apostles, however, braved the ridicule. Most of these were people who had learned the sport in Europe or had been to the winter carnivals at Dartmouth and Lake Placid, New York. The little

band persuaded the Boston and Maine Railroad in 1931 to run a special Sunday train from Boston to New Hampshire's White Mountains. At first the train had a thin passenger list, but by the middle of the season the experiment had become so successful that the astonished railroad officials were putting on two and three sections. That winter the *Boston Evening Transcript* printed a weekly ski chart called "Old Man Winter," which was the first page of its kind to appear in any American newspaper. Now the rush was on. The next winter every railroad running North was taking skiers to the White Mountains and the Adirondacks. Trains left Boston and New York in ten sections, carrying as many as 1,500 skiers, where a year before they had taken an average of 200.

Skiing got its greatest boost after the Winter Olympic games of 1932, held at Lake Placid. For the first time Americans saw experts from all over the world, and the sport caught their fancy. Up to that time there had been little downhill skiing and no slalom in this country. After the Olympics, the demand for downhill skiing resulted in the building of hundreds of miles of trails in New England and New York and, as the craze swept West, in the Rockies and the Sierras. Ski tows and aerial tramways followed; winter resorts opened up; villages awakened from hibernation to become snowy boom towns; European instructors by the score came here to establish schools; sporting-goods manufacturers reported sales of skiing equipment at the head of the list. No sport ever grew as fast as skiing did in the thirties. What had been almost wholly a spectator sport in 1930, when small crowds watched the suicidal acts of ski jumpers, became in less than ten years an all-participating sport.

Sonja Henie gave winter sports, and figure skating in particular, a lift, when she came here in 1936 as a pro to stage her first ice carnival. The twenty-two-year old "Norwegian Doll" brought with her the almost unbelievable record of three Olympic titles, ten world championships, and fourteen Norwegian and European titles. She won her first Olympic crown in 1928 when she was fourteen, won again in 1932, and after her 1936 triumph made her professional debut in New York. An instant success, the blond Norse girl had charm and beauty as well as skating ability. Her annual tours and movie appearances brought her millions and started a boom in figure skating and ice carnivals.

The most spectacular athletic event is the ski jump, comparable in many ways to the pole vault in track and field. Both involve a fast start, a take off, a leap, and a landing, and both require courage, agility, and form. Torger Tokle (above), a transplanted Norwegian, had all those qualities and more when he was making his record leaps in the early forties. The ski jump is judged not only on distance; courage, control, and form, or gracefulness, also count for points. Tokle, who ranks among the finest ski artists, could jump out of sight with the gracefulness of a soaring bird. He broke the American record in 1941 with a 273-foot leap and bettered it himself the next year, and again in 1942, with a jump of 289 feet. A leap of that distance means a take-off speed of about 65 miles an hour. The flight through the air lasts between three and four seconds, during which the jumper is about seventy feet off the ground at the highest point. Then comes the terrific shock of landing. It takes courage, and Tokle had it. He died in combat in the mountains of Italy in 1944 with a U.S. ski-patrol force.

The football Bowl business began innocently enough way back in 1902, when Michigan sent a team to the Coast to play Stanford at Pasadena in connection with the Tournament of Roses Festival. The annual Pasadena splurge (note below) has always been attended by a parade of rose-covered floats and decorated by a carnival queen. The pioneer Bowl game (Michigan won, 49–0) was merely part of the spectacle, and no more Bowl games were played until 1916. One reason for the lapse was the fact that Stanford and California switched from football to rugby during those years. But when football returned to the Coast, so did the Bowl games, and they have been played every year since 1916. Until the thirties, the California promoters had no competition. Then rival boosters, sensing the tremendous profits in the post-season racket, gave birth to a litter of Bowl games, such as the Orange, Sugar, Sun, and Cotton Bowl games. Within a few years a grand total of fifty•Bowl games were reached, about the number played today. Amazing bowls were invented—such as the Oil Bowl and the Gator Bowl. Much criticism has been leveled at the Bowl games on the grounds that they are plainly commercial propositions staged to make money for local merchants and cooperating colleges. Notable exceptions are the All-Star Shrine Games played annually at San Francisco and Miami for the benefit of crippled children.

The last time an Ivy League team played in the Rose Bowl was in 1934, when Lou Little (right) brought his Columbia Lions out to the Coast to meet Stanford. Columbia had a good team but not a great one, having suffered a 20–0 defeat by Princeton. Stanford, with All-Americans Bobby Grayson, Bill Corbus, and Bob Reynolds, was the overwhelming choice to slaughter what Coast sports-writers ridiculed as a "nice little Eastern team." The Bowl was only half-filled when the gigantic Indians lined up against the Lions on the rain-soaked field. It was soon evident that the visitors were going to be no push-overs. Time and again the Indians got within scoring distance only to be turned back. Then, in the second quarter, came the key play, now famous as KF-79, when Al Barabas (See above), on a spinner, drifted around left end, while the Stanford players stood wondering what had become of the ball. Barabas loped the seventeen yards to the goal line untouched. The point was kicked, and it was 7–0 in favor of Columbia—and that was the score at the final whistle. The well-drilled Lions had put over the most stunning upset in Rose Bowl history.

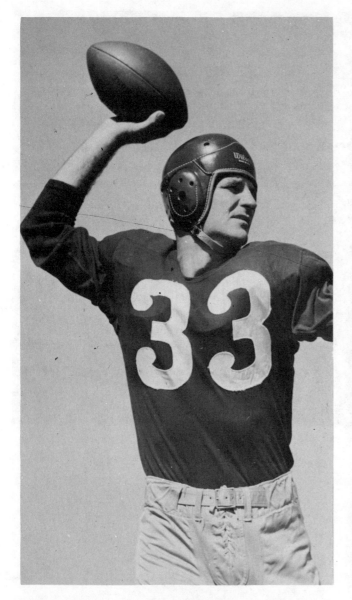

Professional football came of age in the twenties following Red Grange's switch from the college game. It had been played on and off since 1895 with no great success, but, with the organizing of the National Football League on a sound basis in 1922, the long struggle, with the help of Grange, was about to end. On these pages are shown four outstanding college stars who went on to distinguish themselves in the pro game during the 1930–50 period.

Above is quarterback Sammy Baugh, of Texas Christian and the Washington Redskins. A magnificent kicker and defensive back, Slingin' Sammy was even more brilliant as a passer.

When the *New York Evening Sun* invited the members of its All-America team to a dinner in New York in 1929, only ten men showed up. This was no surprise to the *Sun*, for the newspaper had picked only ten men for the eleven positions. Bronko Nagurski made it twice—as fullback and tackle—the only time any football player has been so honored. Bronko deserved it, for he ranks as the greatest all-around player of all time. At Minnesota he played tackle, fullback, and end. On the Chicago Bears he was fullback. The giant Minnesota powerhouse could tear a line apart like a runaway tank. There have been better runners, kickers, and passers than the Bronk, but no one has yet come along to match him in all-around ability.

Don Hutson, of Alabama and the Green Bay Packers, was perhaps the finest end on attack the game has ever seen. The rangy 185-pounder was fast as a sprinter and could feint half a team out of position with his sharp turns while racing at top speed. He was generally all by himself when the ball reached him. Hutson had an uncanny ability to estimate the speed of a pass in flight and to get to it at the exact instant. He is paired with Benny Oosterbaan, Michigan's greatest end, on most all-time teams. Hutson had superiors defensively but not as a pass catcher, as his National Football League record testifies. When he retired at the end of the 1945 season, he held all the pass-catching and scoring records: most passes caught, 489; most touchdown passes caught, 101; most touchdowns scored, 105; most yards gained catching passes, 8,010. Don's remarkable record was made during the one-platoon era and he had to take a beating in defensive as well as in offensive play.

Tommy Harmon was a once-in-a-generation halfback who carried the ball for Michigan just before World War II and made fans hearken back to Thorpe, Gipp, and Grange. Harmon was a sixty-minute player who could pass and run with the best. For two seasons (1939–1940) he was on the national honor roll as leading passer and runner. A sensational break-away runner, Tommy reached his peak against California in 1940, when he made touchdown gallops of ninety-four, seventy-two, eighty-six, and eighty yards. Harmon served in the Air Force and returned, with a Purple Heart and a gimpy leg, to play for the Los Angeles Rams. As a pro he was not the standout he had been at Michigan, where he was All-American for two years. Inevitably, compared to Grange, the Illinois redhead was considered by Alonzo Stagg superior to Grange in everything but running. "I'll take Harmon on my team," said Stagg, "and you can have the rest."

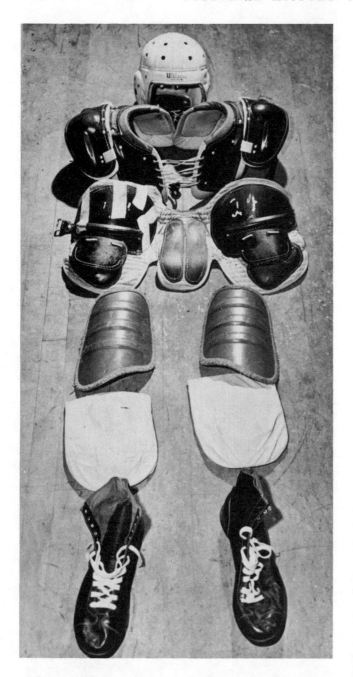

The huddle goes back to 1896, when it was first used in a game between Georgia and Auburn, but it did not come into general use until coach Bob Zuppke introduced it at Illinois in the twenties. One of the first coaches to show it to the East was Herb McCracken of Lafayette. Just before a game during the 1924 season, a rumor reached the campus that the opposing team knew the Lafayette signals. It was too late to change them, so McCracken told his quarterback to call his teammates into a huddle and to give them the signals before each play. The maneuver was so successful that Lafayette continued to call signals from a huddle. By the end of the twenties the system was universally used. Since 1876, when football rules were first adopted, the game has seen more changes than any other. One rule, however, that has never been changed is the one defining the distance between the uprights of the goal posts and the height of the crossbar from the ground. The uprights have always been 18 feet, 6 inches, the crossbar 10 feet high. Throughout all the years, drop kickers and placement kickers have been aiming at this unchanged target.

The modern football uniform looks like something a knight would wear for an encounter with a dragon —and costs almost as much. In the early nineties, shinguards, rubber noseguards, and helmets made their appearance. Shinguards were necessary because of the free use of feet in mass formations, and noseguards were a protection against slugging. Both disappeared along with the mass plays, but helmets were retained. For years they were made of padded leather. Today's tough-fibred headgear and shoulder pads are thought by many to cause more injuries than they prevent.

As these pictures demonstrate, there has been no change in the basic purpose of the game: to advance the ball when on the offensive and to prevent it from being advanced by the opposition. On the right is a picture of a Yale–Princeton game drawn in 1879 by A. B. Frost. Below, a photo taken in 1935 of the Chicago Bears All-Star game. A span of fifty-six years separates these two games. During that time there have been so many changes that the old game would scarcely be recognized today—except for the fundamental purpose: to stop the man with the ball.

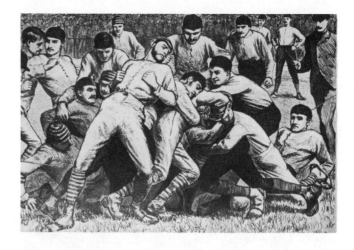

The Army had things its own way in 1944, '45, and '46, when Felix (Doc) Blanchard (above) and Glenn Davis (above, right) were carrying the ball for the Black Knights. Blanchard, the "Mr. Inside" of the remarkable combination, was a big, bruising fullback who could run one hundred yards in ten flat, punt fifty yards, and rip apart the middle of a line. He could sweep the flanks, too.

But that was the job for Davis, "Mr. Outside," who was one of the fastest backs ever seen. Davis might well have been an Olympic sprinter. He was officially clocked at 9.8 seconds for the century as a California high school boy. He won several sprints at West Point but preferred baseball, at which he excelled. Davis scorched the gridirons in 1944, when he made a total of twenty touchdowns, most of them with runs of thirty yards or more.

No doubt Army had the edge in manpower during the last two war years, but their opponents were not the cripples and children the subway alumni liked to say they were. The Army teams of that period would have stood up at any time. In 1945 there were five West Pointers named on the Associated Press All-American. Both Blanchard and Davis made it for three years running. The forgotten man was Arnold Tucker, a quarterback who would have been sensational as a broken-field runner on a team that didn't boast a Blanchard and a Davis. For three years the Black Knights did not taste defeat. They manhandled their old foe, Notre Dame, 59–0 in 1944 and 48–0 the next year. Then in 1946, with the Irish at full strength, came the game of games, when both teams came to the Yankee Stadium with a clean slate. Here was a battle between the nation's two top teams. They were so even neither team could get anywhere, and the game ended in a scoreless tie. In the above picture of that game, Notre Dame's Johnny Lujack hands the ball to Emil Sitko, as Davis (41) and Tucker (17) back up the Army line. Army withdrew from the Notre Dame schedule in 1948.

Babe Didrikson (Mrs. George Zaharias) won more titles in more sports than any other athlete, man or woman. The above picture shows her (second from the right) when she first burst into international fame by winning the 80-meter hurdles in the 1932 Olympics. In the same games, she won the javelin throw and placed second in the high jump after her record jump was disallowed. The Babe was nineteen then. Fifteen years later (opposite page), she came home with the British Women's Amateur golf title to complete a string of sixteen straight golf victories in tournament play. The rangy Texas girl turned pro after the 1932 Olympics and toured the country, starring in a variety of sports. In basketball she was named five times for all-American honors while playing with the Dallas Golden Cyclones; she played baseball for the bearded House of David team, and gave exhibitions in billiards. She excelled at everything she did. Returning to the amateur ranks, she soon became the best woman golfer in the world. Five times between 1932 and 1950 she has been voted the Female Athlete of the Year. The Babe ranked with the greatest all-around athletes of any era. She died of cancer in 1956 at the age of forty-two.

The picture on this page shows Max Schmeling winning the heavyweight championship of the world —on the canvas from a questionable low blow delivered by Jack Sharkey in the fourth round. At that time (June 12, 1930) the title was vacant. After Tunney's defeat of Dempsey in Chicago, the Marine stopped Tom Heeney, a mediocre Australian, and then retired. With the title open, an elimination tournament brought together Sharkey and Schmeling, the best of an ordinary lot. It was then that the German, after being on the receiving end for four rounds, took a punch near the belt line and sank groaning to the floor. The claim of foul was allowed. In a return bout two years later Sharkey outpointed the German in a dull contest that could have been called either way. Thus, Schmeling became the first man in ring history to win the championship lying down and to lose it standing up. There was worse fare ahead for ring fans. In the offing was the monstrous Italian freak, Primo Carnera, a mob-controlled palooka who knew nothing about fighting. His tank tour, in which he scored twenty-two straight "victories," was the rawest deal in ring history. Boxing writers, to their everlasting shame, played along with the racketeers who owned the Italian oaf. (Only Dan Parker and one or two other sports writers raised a voice against the obvious fraud.) In time Carnera did learn the rudiments of boxing and was matched to fight Sharkey for the title. The bout held on June 29, 1933, at the Garden's Long Island Bowl, ended with Sharkey stretched on the canvas in the sixth round. The blow that lowered him was seen by few. The "invisible punch" put the crown on Carnera's head.

When Carnera and Max Baer (on the scales) met at the weighing-in before their championship bout, Max amused himself by plucking hairs from the Italian's chest. "She loves me, she loves me not," grinned Baer. That night he knocked Primo down twelve times and stopped him in the eleventh round.

While Baer was sitting on his newly acquired throne in 1934, a twenty-year-old colored boy from Detroit, fighting under the name of Joe Louis (above), blasted his way to the top of the amateur ranks by winning the International Golden Gloves light-heavyweight championship. His record made fight managers pop-eyed; fifty wins out of fifty-four battles, all but seven by knockouts. On July 4th of that year, less than a month after Baer had won his crown, Joe fought his first professional fight and flattened his man in the first round. This was the beginning of a string of short knockout victories which brought Joe's name to the front throughout the Middle West. The East was soon to hear about him—and see him. Meanwhile the heavyweight situation was becoming involved. Baer lost his title in a surprising upset to Jim Braddock, a washed-up battler whose record showed twenty fights in the losing column. For over two years Braddock sat on his title, refusing to meet Schmeling, although he had signed to fight him. The German carried out his part of the contract by actually showing up in ring togs at the Garden Bowl for the "phantom fight." Nobody was there. All this was of no concern to Louis, who kept rolling along.

New York fans were anxious to get a look at the brown-skinned puncher when he came East in the Spring of 1935 to take on Carnera. Louis was just old enough to vote, and some thought that Carnera, with a weight pull of sixty pounds, might be able to halt the inexperienced youngster. What they saw made them forget all about Baer and Braddock— a superb fighting machine, a combined boxer-fighter who punched so fast and accurately that they could scarcely follow the course of his blows. Joe didn't really open up until the sixth round, when he landed a terrific right to Carnera's head. The grotesque Italian toppled over slowly but managed to get to his feet. There was a look of terror on his face as he rose. He never dreamed anyone could hit that hard. Joe brought him down for good a moment later. (The picture below shows Carnera in his corner after the knockout.)

Baer was next. In the fourth round the ex-champion took the count sitting down (see below), before 88,000 people. The next man in line was Paulino Uzcudun, a rugged Basque, who lasted four rounds. Then came Charley Retzlaff in Chicago. One round for Charley. Max Schmeling was around clamoring for a fight with Braddock in the hope that he could regain his lost title. When the German agreed to take on Louis, no one thought Schmeling had an outside chance. But what ring followers did not know was that success had come too easily for the Brown Bomber. Joe skimped on his training in the belief that he could stop the German easily. The overconfident youngster was ripe for a lesson —and he got it. An astonished crowd saw Schmeling give him a fearful beating and then knock him out in the twelfth round. It was a lesson Joe never forgot.

Schmeling's stunning K.O. of Louis made the German the logical contender for Braddock's title, but he was given the runaround. (It was during this period that Schmeling trained for the "phantom fight.") Less than a month after the Schmeling upset, Louis was back in the ring again, this time against Jack Sharkey, who was trying to stage a comeback. It wasn't much of a fight. Joe gave the ex-champion a cruel beating and knocked him out in the third round. The Brown Bomber had learned his lesson. He trained faithfully, fought often, and never again underestimated an opponent. In due time he was matched with Braddock for the title (June 22, 1937). It was a foregone conclusion that Joe would win. He did—in the eighth round—but not before he had been dumped for a count of two by the aging Braddock.

This picture shows Joe stepping clear of the badly battered Schmeling while referee Arthur Donovan directs the champion to a neutral corner. Of all Joe's fights, this was the high note, the sweetest moment of his ring career. It was a real grudge fight. Joe hated the German who had made him wait two years for a return match and who had meanwhile become a devoted Nazi. And Schmeling was the one man who had beaten him. It was no cautious Shufflin' Joe who came out of his corner when the bell rang. Before the clang had died away, Joe was at his man with a savage attack. It was a butchery. The German went down three times and was on all fours, beaten to a pulp, when Donovan stopped the slaughter. It had taken Joe two minutes and four seconds to avenge the defeat he had suffered two years before.

While ring fans were hailing Joe Louis as one of the greatest heavyweights in history, another colored fighter was capturing headlines on the sports pages with his remarkable feats. He was Henry Armstrong (below, facing the camera), a human dynamo from California, who collected three world championships and held them simultaneously. Armstrong was a tireless, two-handed puncher with abnormal strength and endurance. He swarmed over his opponents, smothered them with blows that came from all angles. Hurricane Hank, weighing 124 pounds, won the first of his three titles in 1937 when he knocked out featherweight champion Petey Sarron in six rounds. Seven months later he outpointed Barney Ross for the welterweight title, and on August 17, 1938, he dropped down a class to win the lightweight championship from Lou Ambers. Thus, the doughty little Negro became the first man in ring history to hold three titles at the same time. Bob Fitzimmons won the world middleweight, heavyweight and light heavyweight titles in that order, but he did not hold them simultaneously. Hurricane Hank's feat of wearing three crowns at once will probably never be duplicated.

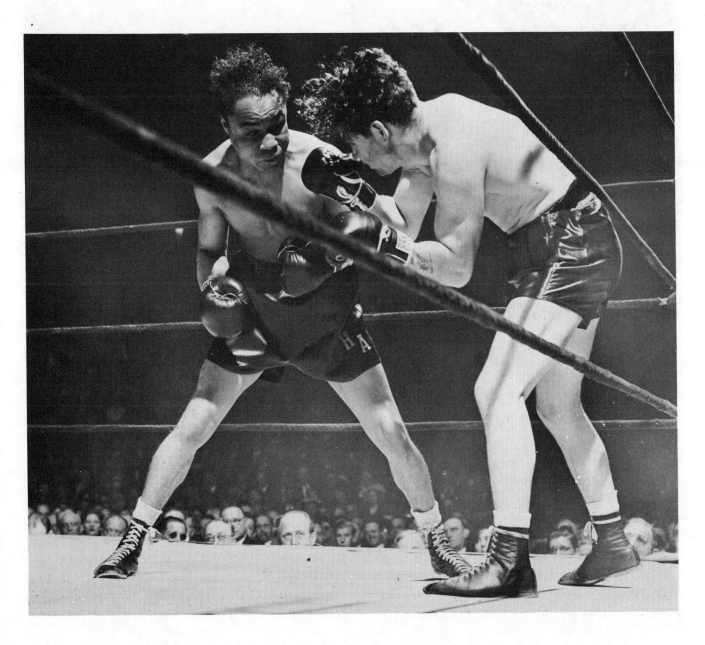

Dr. Naismith's game, intended to fill the need for a winter gymnasium sport, became a big-league affair in 1934, when sports writer Ned Irish introduced it to New York's Madison Square Garden. Before then it had been confined to college gyms and armories. It was an over night success at the Garden. (The picture above shows a standing-room-only crowd of 18,000 at the C.C.N.Y.–Arizona game, December 1950.) At first Irish staged eight programs over a three-month period. Fans clamored for more, and Irish responded with a fourteen-game slate, then with the National Invitation Tournament in 1938, a post-season schedule supposedly featuring the twelve best teams in the nation. An invitation meant thousands of dollars in the till for the privileged colleges. Coaches fought each other to put teams in the Garden and combed the country for basketball talent. Trouble was ahead.

An athletic phenomenon known as the "goon" came into existence when basketball became big business. A more elegant word is "ectomorph," meaning a lanky, linear person such as Ed Macauley (above), whose six-foot, eight-inch frame helped St. Louis University win the N.I.T. in 1948.

As the Garden schedule expanded, and attendance mounted, the gamblers moved in. The sure-thing operators, recognizing basketball's possibility as a betting medium, instituted a handicapping method in which points were awarded to the better teams. A Minneapolis bookmaking house supplied the nation with point odds, and the road was open for the fix. Meanwhile Irish's promotional idea caught on in Philadelphia, Boston, Chicago, and San Francisco. The University of Kentucky and North Carolina State College built basketball arenas on the grandiose Garden scale. Some of the traditional games were moved from tiny college gyms to spacious arenas. Alert sports writers saw the danger and issued warnings, which were ignored. Then in January, 1945, the long-expected scandal broke when five Brooklyn College players admitted having taken bribes to throw a game. That was only the start. In time, four other greater-New York college teams were revealed to have crooked players. It could happen only in New York, said basketball coaches in the hinterland. Then Bradley University and Toledo fell by the wayside. They were followed by Kentucky on evidence revealed in 1951. In all, the record showed eight colleges and some forty players involved. The nation was stunned, as were the coaches, who professed that they had had no idea of what was going on.

The biggest sports event in the world, from the standpoint of participation, is the American Bowling Congress Tournament. Every year some 30,000 bowlers gather at the site selected by the A.B.C. and spend three months rolling balls night and day down brand-new alleys at brand-new pins. The tournament is for the low and the mighty, the expert and the dub, and the man who wins the Singles crown must conquer the largest field in sports. He is the longest shot in competitive athletics, for past performances count for little at the annual carnival. (Left) Bowling in the 1880's.

The biggest drawing-card in bowling was Chesty Joe Falcaro (right), one of the few who brought color to the ordinarily monotonous business of rolling a ball at pins. Joe never won an A.B.C. title, but he had an average of 196 in twenty-one tournaments and was the best match-bowler of them all. When there was any money at stake in a challenge match of forty games or more, he was unbeatable. Although he was occasionally whipped in short matches, no one could take him in a marathon. Joe had unlimited self-esteem and a flair for theatrics. He would dance, leap about, holler at the ball, and put body English on his shots. He would inform the gallery in a loud aside that he was going to knock the brains out of his opponent. Instead of irritating the clients, Joe had them on his side, because he almost always came through. With the exception of Willie Hoppe, no athlete in this century remained on top as long as Falcaro. He rolled his first ball as a nine-year-old pinboy. Joe was the talk of the alleys while still in his teens when he beat Jimmy Smith, the recognized world champion, in a challenge match. For over twenty-five years he stayed on top. In all, he rolled over a million games, scoring 300 in more than sixty of them. (A 300 game is comparable to a no-hitter in baseball.) Of the country's twenty-million bowlers, Joe was the king pin.

In this picture, a group of admirers hoist aloft Andy Varipapa upon his winning of the All-Star National Match-Game Championship in Chicago in 1946. This tournament, conducted under a complicated scoring system, draws a select group of top-notch keglers and is considered to be a truer test than the mass-attended A.B.C. carnival. The winner of the A.B.C. Singles is often an unknown who has a hot three-game streak on a pair of alleys. The Match-Game contestants have to throw sixty-four games across the alleys in a nine-day marathon of bowling.

Ned Day, Joe Wilman, and Buddy Bomar are some of the famous all-year bowlers who have copped the National Match-Game Championship. But their names do not appear in the winning column of the A.B.C. Singles. Varipapa is one of the few who has won the Match Game title twice. Like his old rival, Joe Falcaro—both were born in Italy and grew up in New York—Andy is a fearsome competitor in match play. Millions have seen him in movie shorts as an instructor and trick-shot artist. Both Andy and Joe are charter members of New York's Bowling Hall of Fame.

The winter version of bowling (with shuffleboard overtones) is the ancient Scottish game of curling. The picture below shows a *bonspiel* on Stormont Loch, Scotland, with over 250 curlers on the ice. On the right is the standard forty-four-pound stone which curlers send slithering down the ice in an attempt to nudge an opponent's stone out of the scoring circle. As the stone progresses, two members of the four-man team stand with brooms in hand, ready to sweep away any dirt or pieces of ice that might impede its course. The sport, which is more a sociable gathering than an athletic contest, was first played here on an organized basis in 1840 in Detroit. There are now about 4,000 curlers in the United States, most of them concentrated in clubs in New England and the Middle West.

237

Above, Charley Grimm, manager of the Cubs, Joe McCarthy, Yankee pilot, and President Roosevelt pose for cameramen before the opening game of the 1932 World Series. This was McCarthy's second year with the Yankees, his first as a pennant winner. McCarthy was a baseball curiosity. He had never worn a big-league uniform during his twenty-year playing career, and when he was elevated from the minors in 1926 to lead the Cubs, great was the surprise in the baseball world. His five-year tenure in Chicago was so successful, however, that Yankee-owner Ruppert grabbed him when he was set free. In New York McCarthy was to have one of the most successful careers of any manager in history.

This is the Babe calling his shot at Wrigley Field, the most magnificent gesture ever made on a baseball diamond. This illustration, which appeared in Esquire magazine, shows the Babe in the fifth inning of the third game of the 1932 World Series. It had been a grudge Series. Joe McCarthy, who had been fired by Cub owner Bill Wrigley two years before, was looking for revenge. The whole Yankee team was sore at the Cubs because they had voted the former Yankee shortstop, Mark Koenig, only a half share in the Series. (He had come to the Cubs in midseason but his brilliant play enabled them to win the pennant.) The Bronx Bombers won the first two games in New York and then went to Chicago. In the fifth inning the score was tied at four-all when Ruth came up to be greeted by a barrage of abuse from the Chicago bench. It was then that the Babe became the perfect showman. He took a strike and then defiantly pointed to the centerfield bleachers.

He took another strike and again indicated his target by pointing. The Cubs jeered from the bench. On the next pitch Ruth took a swing as only he could swing and the ball sailed to the deepest part of the center field bleachers, exactly to where he had pointed. He was laughing so hard as he trotted around the bases that he had trouble getting home. The Babe was then in his nineteenth year in major league ball and was beginning to slip. Only two more years were left him as a Yankee and then after a short season with the Braves he was through. The records that he could look back on would fill pages—fifty-four official major league records established or equalled. Everything he did was on the grand scale. He was paid the largest salary, drew the longest suspension and suffered the largest fine ever assessed on any ball player. His name was famous in lands where the game was never played. And he was a showman. Ask the Cubs.

Under the leadership of Joe McCarthy, the Yankees took over the League—and practically the game itself—for the best part of fifteen years. "Great players make great managers," Miller Huggins used to say. McCarthy had great players, two of whom are shown on this page. On the left is Bill Dickey, best catcher in Yankee history and one of the all-time greats. Below is Joe DiMaggio, a manager's dream player, whose superb hitting, throwing, and defensive play in center field puts him in a class with the best. There were other stars on McCarthy's talent-rich club: Red Rolfe, Frank Crosetti, Tony Lazzeri, Joe Gordon, Tommy Henrich, Red Ruffing and Lefty Gomez—and, of course, Lou Gehrig. With such players the Bombers dominated the game so completely that it became monotonous to anyone but a Yankee rooter. In McCarthy's fifteen-year Yankee career (1931–1945), his clubs won eight pennants, seven World Series, finished second four times, and were never out of the first division.

On this page are shown some of the members of the Gas-House Gang, St. Louis' contribution to the game in the thirties when the Yankees were top dog in the other league. Putting on a show for their new boss, Mike Gonzalez (center), who replaced Frisch in 1938, are, from left to right: Pepper Martin, Frenchy Bordagaray, Bob Weiland, Gonzalez, Lon Warneke, Fibber McGee, and Don Padgett. In the picture on the right, Dizzy Dean twists the Tiger's tail after he and his brother Paul pitched the four winning games needed to beat the Detroit Tigers in the 1934 Series. The swashbuckling Cards always played colorful, aggressive baseball. They were the one bright spot in the National League for twenty years (1926–1946), when they won nine pennants and six World Series. The unterrified Cards were the underdogs in virtually every October classic, but the best any American League club could do was to break even with them. (The Cards beat the Yankees in 1926 and 1942, lost to them in 1928 and 1943; they split with the A's in 1930 and 1931, winning the second encounter.) The other three American League teams they met—the Tigers, Browns, and the expensive Red Sox—all went down to defeat. If it hadn't been for the Cards, the National League would have reached near-minor league status.

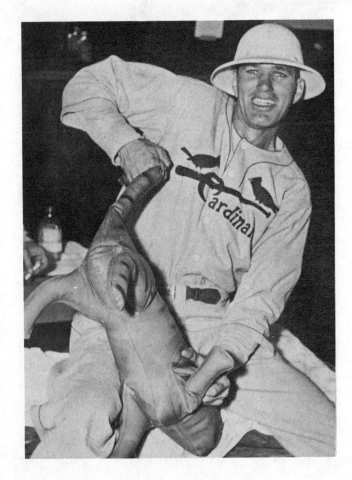

Two speedballers of the lively ball era (Lefty Grove, above, and Bob Feller, right) furnish fans with the perennial dispute over which was the faster. It would take an electric eye to settle the question, but there was no doubt that both could throw an "aspirin tablet," a phrase coined by some unknown batter in describing what a speedball looked like as it came up to the plate. Grove finished his career with the Red Sox in 1941 with an even 300 victories, which gave him the highest won-and-lost percentage (.680) of any pitcher in the Hall of Fame. The flame-thrower, who had his best years with the A's, always maintained that with the dead ball he would have won 500 games. His reasoning: in the pre-Ruth era, when a half-dozen homers would lead the league, a pitcher could use a dirty or scuffed ball and employ trick deliveries. He had much more in his favor in those days. Since Grove, however, two hurlers have won 300 games or more: Warren Spahn and Early Wynn. Bob Feller with 285 victories almost certainly would have made the 300 Club if the war hadn't interrupted his baseball career for four years.

On this page are three ball players who never wore any other uniform but that of the New York Giants. They started under McGraw, continued after he left, and, when Mel Ott (below) finished his playing career in 1947, it marked the end of a long line of McGraw players. On the right is Bill Terry (pointing) and below him is Carl Hubbell (left) with his battery mate, Gus Mancuso. (The catcher came to the Giants after the manager's exit and was never a McGrawman.) But the other three were of the old breed of Giants—Ott, who served twenty-two years with the club and hit the most homers, batted in the most runs, and scored the most runs in National League history; Terry, who rivalled Gehrig as a hitter and was more skillful around the bag; and King Carl Hubbell, the Meal Ticket, who was the best Giant hurler since Mathewson and who put together twenty-four consecutive victories, the longest string on record. They won pennants for the Giants in 1933, '36, and '37, and then the fortunes of the club ran out. Not for fourteen years did the Giants see another flag—not until 1951, when Bobby Thomson's miraculous homer in the ninth inning of the third and deciding play-off game with the Dodgers reminded old-timers of the days of the old McGrawmen.

The National Baseball Museum and Hall of Fame at Cooperstown, New York, opened its doors on June 12, 1939, to enshrine forever thirteen immortals who had been chosen by a poll of baseball writers. This was the first of many sports shrines to follow. Since then, football, golf, trotting, and hockey have honored their great performers in like manner. But Cooperstown led the way. In 1908 organized baseball announced that the game had originated there in 1839, and a century later the shrine was opened in commemoration of the event. The fact that evidence has since come to light which refutes Cooperstown's claim has caused some anguish among the literal-minded. But to baseball lovers the country over, it makes little difference. The game was first played by schoolboys on pastures and village greens, and it is appropriate that the shrine should be located in a typical country village. Such a place is Cooperstown, where Abner Doubleday is supposed to have brought order to the scrambled game of rounders that later became baseball. It is there that the relics and records of the game have been and will be carefully preserved for the great crowds who visit the shrine every year. Through contributions of many famous players and fans from all over the country, the building became so crowded with priceless relics that an addition was made in 1951 which almost doubled the size of the original structure. A few years later the building was again enlarged and a special wing was added for the enshrined Hall of Famers.

All the living players originally chosen for the Hall of Fame were present at the opening. They are shown below, minus Ty Cobb, who got there too late to sit for this picture. Standing, left to right, are: Hans Wagner, Grover Alexander, Tris Speaker, Nap Lajoie, George Sisler, and Walter Johnson. In the front row, in the same order: Eddie Collins, Babe Ruth, Connie Mack, and Cy Young. Wee Willie Keeler and Christy Mathewson were honored among the original thirteen, but they had passed on by that time. Ty Cobb's tardiness caused the old-timers to comment that this was nothing new. The Georgia Peach was always late for spring training, they said. "But not late," said Eddie Collins, "on the base paths." It was Collins who said, when the players were introduced as they emerged one by one between the bronze doors of the Museum, "I couldn't have been a bat boy for this bunch." (The modest second baseman played major-league ball for twenty-five years, had a lifetime batting average of .333, and was one of the few honest players on the infamous White Sox team of 1919.) If he could have been only the bat boy, think of the others: Old Pete Alexander, winner of 373 games; George Sisler, a .420 hitter one year with a .340 lifetime average—and so on through the list. Never before had such a wealth of baseball talent come together as when this picture was taken.

The race that everyone was waiting for finally came off when Seabiscuit, the ugly duckling from the Pacific Coast, and War Admiral, handsome winner of the Triple Crown, met in a match race at Pimlico on November 1, 1938. The Biscuit was an old campaigner who had started eighty-three times, had gone lame, and then had come back to win several stake races. He had had his ups and downs ever since he was picked up by C. S. Howard for $8,500, a discard from the Wheatley Stable. In contrast, War Admiral, the one-to-four favorite, had an almost perfect record. The son of Man O' War was undefeated in eight starts in 1937 and, as winner of the Kentucky Derby, the Preakness, and the Belmont, was named the Horse of the Year. The old

Biscuit, now back in form, had never met his Eastern rival. For the dream race, each carried 120 pounds over the mile-and-three-sixteenths distance. And it was a dream race. Jockey George Woolf (above, in the lead on Seabiscuit with Charley Kurtsinger trailing) whipped his mount away from the starting post and took the lead by a length. He held it until the backstretch, when Kurtsinger decided to ask War Admiral for his best. The Man O' War colt responded with a bound. His nose showed in front as they pounded down the homestretch. Then the Biscuit drove forward and pulled away. War Admiral under the whip could do no more, and the Western horse came to the wire four lengths in front.

The buggy crowd didn't care much about the doings on the turf between Seabiscuit and War Admiral. They had a champion of their own in Greyhound (below), the fastest trotter in history. The grey gelding was virtually unbeatable in the thirties. After winning the Hambletonian in 1935, he started in on a record-breaking career. He equalled the old mile mark of 1:56¾ and kept hacking away at it until he got it down to 1:55¼, which is comparable to a man doing a four-minute mile. No other trotter threatened Greyhound's time in twenty-five years. The pacer, Adios Butler, turned in a 1:54 3/5 mile in 1960, however. Harness racing, despite its rural origins has become a big-time, city sport with some 600 trotting tracks in operation.

Ellsworth Vines, shown here as a tennis player and golfer, flashed briefly on the courts after Tilden's change-over to the pro game. The crop that followed furnished such good performers as John Doeg, George Lott, Frank Shields, and Wilmer Allison, but none excited the hopes of tennis fans as Vines did. The lanky Californian looked like another Tilden for a couple of years. He came out of nowhere in 1931 to win the National Championships at the age of twenty, repeated this feat the following year, and added the Wimbledon title. Tilden was twenty-seven when he won his first National Championship and thirty-six when he won his last one, in 1929. Vines seemed to be on the threshold of a long career. But he was no Tilden. He went into a bad slump in 1933 and then turned pro. Later he became a golf pro and toured the circuit with no great success.

Here, Don Budge (left) shakes hands with the English champion Fred Perry. Like Red McLoughlin, Budge was a carrot-topped Californian with a smashing, dynamic game. His peak year was 1937, when he won the American, British, French, and Australian championships, the Grand Slam of tennis.

On the opposite page is Don Budge, the only tennis player of recent years who could be mentioned in the same breath with Tilden. The redhead had a fine all-around game, featured by the most explosive backhand in court history. This picture shows him at Wimbledon in 1937, in the midst of his memorable battle with Baron Gottfried von Cramm in the Davis Cup challenge round. It was undoubtedly the greatest match ever played. It was tennis perfection, so flawless that each man earned more points than he lost on errors, and there wasn't a soft shot in the entire five-set match. In the final set, von Cramm flashed to a 4–1 lead, but Budge pulled even, and it then went to 5-all and 6-all. Budge, the fighter, finally broke through service. Match point came and went, came and went. For the sixth time Budge held match point. Then he served with projectile force, but von Cramm miraculously got his racquet on the ball. After a fiery exchange, the German shot one to the left side behind Budge. The redhead turned, raced at full speed, and blasted the ball just over the net. It passed von Cramm like a bullet, and the match was over.

By winning that match—the fifth and deciding one between the United States and Germany—the American team earned the right to meet Great Britain for the Davis Cup. The American 1937 team is shown below. From left to right flanking the official with the cup are Budge, Frank Parker, Bitsy Grant. and Gene Mako. After the dramatic match between Budge and von Cramm, the final round play was somewhat of an anticlimax. Budge won his two singles matches against Bunny Austin and Charles Hare; Parker split with the two Englishmen, defeating Hare; and Budge and Mako won the doubles for a 4–1 Cup victory. The goblet was at last back in our possession after ten years, during which time France had had it for six years and England for four. It was not to stay here long, however. The two-man Australian team of Adrian Quist and Jack Bromwich was more than Bobby Riggs, Parker, Jack Kramer, and Joe Hunt could handle in 1939, when the Aussies won 3–2. Old-timers recalled that the last time a two-man team from Down Under (Brookes and Wilding) won the Cup, a world war followed. Was this an omen of another world war?

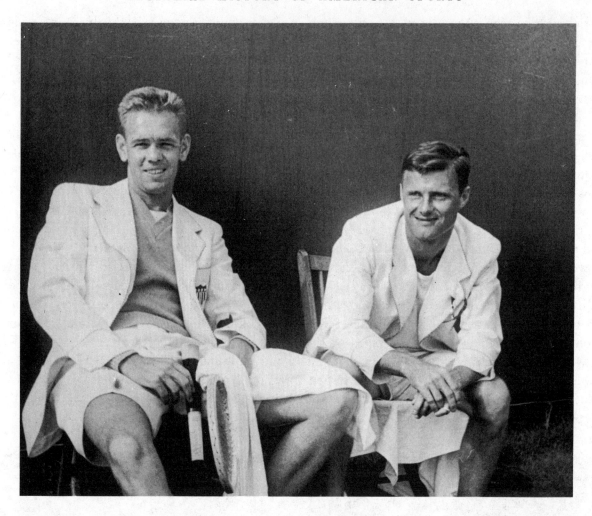

One of the best doubles teams in recent times was the Kramer–Schroeder combination of the forties. The youngsters first came into prominence in 1940 when, while still too young to vote, they won the National Doubles Championship. (Above, on the left, is big Jack Kramer with his partner, Ted Schroeder. The action picture shows them in midcourt.) The pair picked up two more national titles and, as partners and singles players on the Davis Cup teams of 1946 and 1947, were the key men in taking the trophy away from Australia and keeping it here for a while. Of all the nations America has met in the battle for the Cup, Australia has furnished the most opposition. The two countries have battled it out sixteen times, a remarkable record for the land Down Under, whose population is about one twentieth of ours. The team of Kramer and Schroeder, both of whom are United States and Wimbledon Singles Champions, broke up when Kramer turned professional in 1947. In 1950 the goblet went back to Australia again.

For thirteen years Frank Parker tried and failed to win the national crown. Playing a steady though uninspiring game, he was forced to bow to such stars as Vines, Budge, Allison, and Riggs. But in 1944 he finally came through and, to show that it was no accident, repeated the following year.

253

In 1933 Helen Wills Moody (above, wearing visor) was the absolute queen of the courts. She had not been beaten in six years on any court, had not even lost a set. During all those years, Helen Jacobs, also from California, had constantly been walloped by Queen Helen. (Miss Jacobs is shown above with Mrs. Moody; above, right, in action.) Now, in the final at Forest Hills in 1933, the two came together again. The crowd was surprised to see the Queen drop the first set, but when she came back to take the second, 6–3, the usual result was expected. But something happened to Mrs. Moody's game in the final set. She made countless errors, double-faulted and seemed fatigued. With the score 3–0 against her, the end was in sight—and sooner than the crowd of 8,000 expected. For it was then that she suddenly turned to the umpire and told him that she could play no longer. The gallery sat unbelieving as she picked up her blue sweater and started to walk off the court. Miss Jacobs rushed to her to plead that she

continue, but it was no use. She went to the showers, and Miss Jacobs was declared the winner by default. Only once before in the forty-six-year history of the national championship had such a thing happened— when Mlle. Lenglen took a walk on Mrs. Mallory years before on the same court, in a fit of coughing and weeping. Queen Helen, who stated after the match that she had had pains in her back and hip and numbness in her right leg, walked off without so much as a limp. There is little doubt that she was not herself, but everyone who witnessed the match felt that, pain or no pain, she might have stood there and gone through the motions of playing, taking her licking like a good sport, as Helen Jacobs had taken it from her so many times before. And there was some question about the pain, when it was learned that less than an hour after her default she announced that she would play in the doubles final. (Officials talked her out of it.) The Queen later beat her conqueror at Wimbledon on two occasions.

Can the girls take it when the going gets tough? Two who could but didn't have to when they were doubles partners are shown below: Sarah Palfrey Cooke (stroking the ball) and Alice Marble. They won the U. S. Women's Doubles four years running (1937–1940) and a host of other doubles titles. As members of the Wightman Cup teams—the distaff side of the Davis Cup, but with competition limited to England and the United States—the eye-pleasing pair helped bring victory to this country for a decade. Miss Marble, a blond, well-formed Californian, won four singles championships at Forest Hills and one at Wimbledon. The petite Sarah, a Bostonian, was twice U. S. Singles champion, the last time in 1945, when she was the mother of a two-year-old daughter.

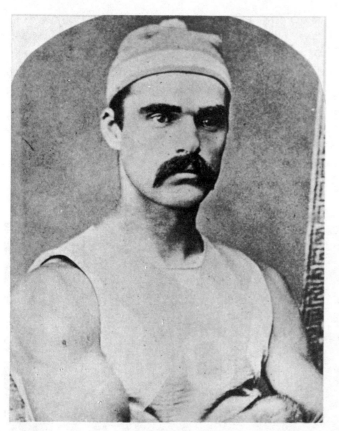

Charles E. (Pop) Courtney (left) turned out so many winning crews in his long coaching career at Cornell (1883–1916) that the University became identified with the sport. Courtney was the finest single-sculls oarsman the country ever produced. At Cornell the "Courtney stroke" made victory a habit. In the two decades after 1895, Courtney sent fifty-nine crews to Saratoga and Poughkeepsie and won thirty-nine races. After his passing, rowing dominance shifted to the West Coast. Washington oarsmen and crews coached by Husky grads have virtually owned the Poughkeepsie regatta since the twenties. (Below, mass crew practice on the West coast.) The Intercollegiate Rowing Association regatta, held at Poughkeepsie, New York, since 1895, was shifted to Marietta, Ohio, for two years (1950–51) but since 1952 it has been held at Syracuse, New York, on Onondaga Lake. The year 1952 was a banner one in college rowing history. It marked the hundredth anniversary of the first Harvard-Yale boat race, which, incidentally, is America's oldest intercollegiate sports event.

Above, a victorious crew tosses the coxswain overboard. The time-honored custom probably stems from the crew's mixed emotions of exuberance at winning and resentment of the cox for getting a free ride. American coxswains have taken a persistent dunking in the Olympics since 1900, when the first eight-oared race was held. Except for England's victories in 1908 and 1912, American crewmen have finished first every time.

Below, John B. Kelly, Jr. (in the scull) is greeted by his father, standing on the bank. The senior Kelly was twice National Amateur single-sculls champion and Olympic winner in 1920. Kelly went to England that year to compete in the Diamond Sculls, the most coveted of rowing titles, but was barred because it was discovered that he had been an artisan. (According to the rigid British rules, a laborer is ineligible. Kelly had worked one summer as a bricklayer while a student at Penn.) A generation later, young Kelly succeeded his father as National Champion (1946) and then went to England with unsoiled hands to win the Diamond Sculls. Gleefully Kelly senior sent the King (George VI) a cap of Kelly green.

The divot-digging game suffered a letdown after Bobby Jones' retirement. As the depression hit with full force, country clubs folded, and crowds dwindled at the big tournaments, several of which were discontinued. In the midst of the doldrums appeared Lawson Little (above), a Stanford graduate who could drive a ball a mile. The burly one with the scowling brow was unknown until 1934, when he went to England and won the Amateur. That fall at Brookline he took the American Amateur. There was talk of another Jones when the following year he astounded golf followers by winning both titles again. No other golfer had ever done that before or had even come close to it—and no one has since. By winning the double-double, Little completed a victory string of thirty-one consecutive matches in championship play, a record that seems as safe as the Grand Slam. Little turned pro in 1936 and had a spotty career for the next few years. In 1940 he won the big one, the U. S. Open at Canterbury, in a playoff with Sarazen. Little was never a crowd-pleaser—too grim and intense—but he was an A-1 golfer.

This picture, taken in April, 1937, shows the gallery around the ninth green of the Augusta National Golf Club course watching the match between Byron Nelson and Wiffy Cox. Of all the major PGA tournaments (some thirty-three in all), the Masters, held annually at Augusta, is the one that golfers, as well as spectators, like best. There is no better course in the world, and no tournament is conducted as well. The field, which rarely exceeds sixty-five, is the Blue Book of golf. Masters' bids go to past Masters' champions, U.S. Open, PGA, and Amateur champions, British Open and Amateur champions, members of the Ryder and Walker Cup teams, the first twenty-four players in the previous Masters and Open, quarter-finalists in the PGA and the Amateur, and a few others. Considered the greatest test in golf, the course was designed by Dr. Alister MacKenzie, with Bobby Jones lending a hand. It was built for Jones by his host of friends, and, upon its completion in 1934, the old champion was made president of the club. On Bobby Jones' "dream course" the Masters tournament is golf at its finest.

Flubbing a putt was nothing unusual for Sammy Snead (above) who once blew the U.S. Open by missing a two-and-a-half footer on the eighteenth green in the playoff (in 1947). A brilliant stylist with one of the smoothest swings ever seen, Snead was a gallery favorite when he was burning up the courses from 1937 to the mid-1950's. He won more tournaments of all kinds than any other golfer. Among them: three P.G.A. championships, three Masters, one British Open, three Canadian Opens and also titles won in Panama, South Africa, Brazil and Argentina. But the U.S. Open always eluded him, although he came tantalizingly close to winning it three times. His most disastrous performance took place in the 1939 Open on the last hole. He needed only a five to win, a six to tie. Sam shot an eight.

While Slamming Sammy Snead was making the headlines in 1937 as golf's newest sensation, Ralph Guldahl (right), a far different type of golfer, was plugging away in a mechanical fashion and winning the big ones. The big Texan, who won two consecutive U.S. Open Championships (1937, 1938), was respected as the fine medal player he was, but his lack of showmanship failed to excite the gallery.

Byron Nelson (above) turned in such a number of record-shattering performances that many experts rated him the equal of the great Bobby. The cool, efficient Texan arrived in 1937 by winning the Masters and reached the summit two years later by taking the Open in a double play-off with Craig Wood and Denny Shute. During the war years, Nelson, rejected by the services, toured the country and won about everything in sight. Playing the most consistent golf ever seen, he scored a record-breaking average of 69.67 strokes per tournament round in 1944. The next year he won nineteen tournaments, eleven in a row. No other golfer ever won so many so decisively or gave Old Man Par such a licking.

Ben Hogan (above) and Byron Nelson were boyhood pals back in the days when they were caddies at the Glenn Garden Course at Fort Worth, Texas. If there was ever any thought among the golfers whose bags they toted that both lads would one day write golf history, it is not recorded. Certainly none would have picked the frail Benny, who was half the size of the other boy. From his earliest years, he was not a natural golfer, never a kid phenom as Jones, Hagen, and Sarazen were. He was undersized and lacked power, but from the start he had a great determination and a capacity for self-control and concentration. No golfer ever spent as much time as Hogan did at improving his game. He would practice daily, hour after hour, until his hands were so badly calloused that he could hardly hold a club. It was not until 1940, when he was twenty-eight, that he really began to move. That year he started out on a prolonged streak that brought him into the money in fifty-six tournaments. That was just the beginning. After his discharge from the Army in 1946, Ben took up where he'd left off and showed the world something it had never seen before.

If America has a Royal Family of Golf, it is the Turnesas, of Westchester County, New York, shown here celebrating brother Willie's capture of the British Amateur. (Willie holds the Cup.) The seven Turnesa brothers acquired so many titles and near-titles over so many years that an index is needed to get them straight. With a nod to Herbert Warren Wind, golf writer of note, who chronicled their achievements, the record follows, as they appear in the picture from left to right:

Doug, winner of Westchester pro tournaments.

Joe, member of the Ryder Cup Team, 1927, 1929; second to Bobby Jones in the 1926 U.S. Open; PGA finalist in 1927; winner of the 1929 News of the World Tournament.

Phil, runner-up in Westchester Open; tied for first in the Fort Lauderdale Open.

Willie, U.S. Amateur Champion, 1938, 1948; winner of British Amateur, 1947; finalist British Amateur, 1949; Walker Cup Team, 1947, 1949. (Willie is the only amateur in the family.)

Mike, Sr., father of the seven boys.

Frank, winner of local Westchester tournaments; noted as an instructor. (Frank died in 1949.)

Mike, Jr., finalist in 1948 PGA (won by Hogan); winner of Westchester Open, 1933, 1941.

The seventh brother, *Jim*, who is not in this picture, was a finalist in the 1942 PGA; third in the U.S. Open, 1948; tied for fourth, U.S. Open, 1949; runner-up in the Masters, 1949, and winner of the 1952 PGA.

All in all, the Turnesas deserve the title as America's Royal Family of Golf.

Ben Hogan was struck down at the peak of his career in 1949 in an auto crash that laid him low for months with a broken pelvis, collar bone, ankle, and rib. For days it was a question whether he would live, then whether he would ever walk. As for playing golf again—that was beyond hope. But Hogan, tough and determined, set out to make it. It took months of doctoring and daily massage before he could take a step and more months before he could limp around a golf course, using a cane. Slowly he mended. Then, sixteen months after the near-fatal crash, history caught up with Hogan. In one of the greatest achievements of competitive sports, with the whole country rooting for him, he won the U.S. Open. Thousands of people who had never seen a golf match or played a round hailed his magnificent comeback. It was typical of Hogan to ask reporters to play down his injuries, to write of him as a golfer, not as a cripple. They wrote of him as a golfer again the next year (1951), when he won the Open for the third time. Could he continue to do the impossible and win the Open for the fourth time the following year? He looked a certain winner when he led the field at the halfway mark at Dallas in 1952. But the heat was too much for little Ben and the closing drive that had characterized his play so often was missing. A sad 79 for his final round dropped him into third place. Undismayed by the defeat, the great champion thundered back the following year by winning the U.S. Open and the British Open. It was Ben's finest year.

The highest honor England can bestow upon a golfer was given Francis Ouimet in 1951 when he was elected Captain of the Royal and Ancient Golf Club at St. Andrews, Scotland. This picture shows the old champion in the act of "driving in" off the first tee in observance of the traditional ceremony. It was exactly eight o'clock in the morning, the traditional moment, when Ouimet took his stance. In front of him, at various distances, St. Andrews caddies were strung out, prepared to pounce on the ball for the gold sovereign traditionally awarded to the retriever. Willie Auchterlonie, winner of the 1893 British Open, teed up the ball. As the clock tolled eight, Ouimet took his swing, and the ball shot 170 yards straight down the fairway. An antique cannon beside the tee boomed a salute before the ball came to earth, and Ouimet was officially Captain, the first American to be so honored. The British agreed that the selection was a happy one. Since 1913, when he won the U.S. Open, until 1949, Ouimet had been a member or the non-playing captain of every U. S. Walker Cup team. No American, not even Bobby Jones, holds a higher place in the hearts of the Royal and Ancient members.

For the first time in thirteen years, Joe Louis (left) appeared as challenger when he fought Ezzard Charles for the heavyweight title on September 27, 1950. Joe had announced his retirement the year before, following his knockout of Jersey Joe Walcott. With the title vacant, Ezzard Charles, a dull, cautious workman, emerged as the best of a sorry field to gain recognition as champion. It was more than Joe could stand. It was more than his admirers could stand, too, when they saw how far Joe had slipped. Charles gave him a systematic drubbing for fifteen rounds to win the decision. "I'll never fight again," said Joe after the fight.

By whipping the Brown Bomber, Ezzard had established beyond question his right to the title. Unexciting as he was, he won every time out. Among his victims was thirty-seven-year-old Jersey Joe Walcott, twice beaten by Charles. When the two met for the third time Walcott in the seventh round caught the champion with a smashing left hook to the jaw and down went Ezzard for the full count. On the opposite page, Walcott (right) is about to let one go at the bewildered Charles. Once more (June 5, 1952) the two went at it again in a slow-motion fifteen rounder in Philadelphia. Favored in the betting to become the first dethroned heavyweight champ to regain his title, an overcautious Charles was outpointed in perhaps the dullest title bout ever staged.

When Jersey Joe Walcott was given a belt emblematic of the world heavyweight championship, he was so overcome that he wept unashamedly before a gathering of sports writers and ring followers in a New York restaurant. It had been a long, hard trail for the old guy. He could look back upon an incredible span of twenty-one years from his first recorded professional fight to the championship. During that time he had known poverty, had given up the ring, and had worked as a garbage collector, a stevedore, and a ditch-digger, at anything to pick up a few dollars for his growing family. Everyone was glad to see old Joe, a deeply religious man, devoted to his family, finally make it—on his fifth try for the championship.

Handing Joe the belt is Nat Fleischer, the walking encyclopedia of fistiana. Recognized as boxing's supreme authority, Fleischer has written some twenty-five-million words on the subject as editor of *Ring* magazine and author of forty-five boxing books, at the latest count. His most monumental work is his *All-Time Ring Record Book*, the result of thirty years' research and seven years' writing. It contains the complete record of every noteworthy battler since Jim Figg, first champion of England in 1713, records over 60,000 bouts, and solemnly lists the first contest on record, Cain vs. Abel. Fleischer revived, in 1922, the tradition of donating belts to champions. No belt gave him greater satisfaction than the one he presented to Jersey Joe.

Joe Louis never should have tried it again. If the beating Ezzard Charles gave him didn't convince him that he was through, his next fight should have. He won it—Cesar Brion was the victim—but Joe looked like a weary old man, and his punch was gone. Now, in October, 1951, he was in there again, this time with Rocky Marciano, a tough, twenty-seven-year-old ex-GI from Brockton, Mass. The picture below shows what happened to Joe in the eighth round. This was the first knockdown. A moment later he got to his feet, but a flurry of blows put him down again, and referee Ruby Goldstein signaled the end of the fight. It was a pathetic end for a man who was one of the greatest fighters of them all. And there have been some great ones, from Sullivan on down: Corbett, the supreme boxing master; Fitzsimmons, the paralyzing puncher; the rugged Jeffries, unbeatable for years; Johnson, the all-around ring craftsman; Dempsey, the savage,

deadly hitter; and Tunney, the most intelligent of all the champions and the first one wise enough to retire at his peak. They were the best, and the Brown Bomber ranks with them. Off his record he shows up better than any. He was the youngest to win the championship up to that time. He held it the longest (twelve years) and he defended it twenty-five times, more often than any other champion. Ten men faced him in return bouts and Joe flattened every one of them, each fight ending more quickly and more convincingly than the previous one. Joe knocked out six heavyweight champions, counting Walcott, who later won the title. From 1937 to 1948, during which he spent four years in the Army, Joe was absolutely supreme. Unfortunately, last impressions linger longer than first ones in the ring. Joe's admirers were saddened to see him keep fighting until age robbed him of his skill and punch. They hoped he would be remembered as the great champion he was.

The indoor pool and the introduction of the crawl stroke in the nineties by Richmond Cavill of Australia changed the sport of swimming from a winter pastime to a major intercollegiate and Olympic sport. Above, the start of the mile at the National AAU Championships in 1950. Won by Yale's John Marshall (fifth from bottom), it was his third victory in the meet.

No college has ever dominated a sport so completely as has Yale since Bob Kiphuth (right) was made swimming coach at New Haven in 1917. In his forty-two years as tank master the Elis won 528 dual meets while losing only twelve. Bob's longest string was from 1945 through 1959 when Yale swam away from 176 opponents without a defeat. His famed three M's of the class of 1953—Marshall, Mc-Clane and Moore—have won Olympic National A.A.U. and Intercollegiate titles. (Below, John Marshall [left], Jim McClane [right].) The other M, Wayne Moore, once described as "the world's greatest third-string swimmer," eventually became their equal. Yale's colors were lowered in the 1952 N.C.A.A. meet by Ohio State with the help of freshmen (barred from intercollegiate competition by Ivy League rules) and their great star, Ford Konno. Subsequently the New Haven Swim Club (Yale's varsity), freshmen and alumni, won the A.A.U. team championship over Ohio State, 113–97, though Konno took the 1,500 meter, 220 and 440 yard events.

Ty Cobb raised a furor in baseball circles when, in a magazine article written in 1952, he said that there were only two players in uniform who could be compared with the men of his day—Stan (The Man) Musial (above, making a hit) and Phil (The Scooter) Rizzuto, Yankee shortstop. Much criticism was directed at Cobb for not picking Joe DiMaggio as one of the two, but no voice was raised in protest over his selection of Musial, the great Cardinal outfielder and first baseman. Stan, when Cobb picked him, was in the middle of his phenomenal twenty-two-year career, which was to end in 1963. He shattered most of Mel Ott's marks and wound up with a total of twenty-nine records, enough to put him in a class with Cobb, Ruth and Wagner. Stan was thrice voted the National League's Most Valuable Player and he was the league batting champion six times.

In the American League Ted Williams (left), the Red Sox problem boy (he used to spit at the press box as he crossed the plate) was batting out a name for himself and getting the highest salary in the game—more than $100,000 a year for a few seasons. Ted hit a mighty .406 in 1941.

In this picture (taken in a World Series game between the Yankees and the Dodgers in 1947), Jackie Robinson plunges into second and topples Phil Rizzuto in an attempt to break up the double play at first. George Stirnweiss, Yankee second baseman, stands on the left. (The Scooter got the ball away in time to complete the double killing.) The year was a significant one for the Yankees in that it ended a three-year pennantless stretch and brought a new manager to the Stadium in Bucky Harris. His reign was a short one, however. Bucky got his walking papers the following season, when the Bombers finished third, only three games behind the Indians, who ended the season in a tie with the Red Sox and beat them in the play-off game. It was win or else

with the Yankee front office, despite Bucky's good record and his popularity with the fans and baseball scribes. But his departure was soon forgotten when Casey Stengel arrived to lead the Yankees to five straight world championships (1949–1953). This was the same Casey who had managed the Dodgers and the Braves for a total of nine years without once seeing the first division. But in New York Casey had DiMaggio, Henrich, Yogi Berra, Vic Raschi, Ed Lopat, and Phil Rizzuto. It was little Phil, one of the smallest men in the majors (5 feet, 6 inches) and Cobb's other favorite, who became the heart of the Yankee infield for eleven years. Dependable and brilliant, Phil could hit (.324 in 1950) and make plays with the skill of the great Honus Wagner.

On these two pages are shown a quartet of fair ones who have distinguished themselves in various sports. Above is Maureen Connolly, who, at sixteen, won the National Women's Singles Championship at Forest Hills in 1951 and by doing so, became the second youngest national champion in the tournament's history. (May Sutton was two months younger when she won the title in 1904.) The following year "Little Mo" triumphed at Wimbledon.

On the left is Florence Chadwick, thirty-two-year-old typist, who set a woman's record in 1950 when she swam the channel from France to England in thirteen hours and twenty minutes, more than an hour faster than Gertrude Ederle's record made in 1926. The next year Miss Chadwick did it again, this time swimming from England to France. She was the first woman to make the round trip.

By winning the Special Slalom in the 1948 Olympic Games, Gretchen Fraser (right) became the first American to win a skiing event in the history of the winter games. Four years later, as team manager of the U.S. Women Skiers at Oslo, she saw Andrea Mead Lawrence, a nineteen-year-old girl from Rutland, Vermont, win two gold medals in the slalom events. The American male skiers have not fared as well. They have yet to win a gold medal.

Another girl who put the boys to shame is Joan Pflueger, who won the Grand American Trapshoot at Vandalia, Ohio, in 1950 in competition against an all-male field. The eighteen-year-old girl from Miami, representing Florida, had to shoot it out against the champions of the other forty-seven states (and Cuba). She broke 100 straight clay pigeons, then won the 75-bird shoot-off against four men. Joan was the first female in the fifty-one-year history of the Grand American Trapshoot to win the championship.

In this picture, Citation leads the field on the turn coming into the home stretch to win the Gold Cup at Belmont in October, 1948. That year, the bay colt's greatest, he won nineteen out of twenty races and earned $709,470, the largest amount any horse ever earned in a single year. When the Triple Crown winner came to the post for the Pimlico Special that fall, none could be found to challenge him, and he picked up $10,000 by breezing around the track all by himself. Turf followers rated him above Man O'War. But bad luck was ahead for big Cy. A sore leg kept him out of racing in 1949 and when he returned to the track a year later as a five-year-old in the handicap division he was beaten four times by the Irish-bred horse Noor. The setbacks were no disgrace, however. In five meetings with Noor, he won once, lost three by giving away more than enough weight to excuse him, and lost the last one when he was unsound. Big Cy went on winning to become the first million-dollar horse, with total earnings of $1,085,760, the highest of all time. He won thirty-two races in forty-five starts and won at any distance from a sprint to two miles. Big Cy was good. So was the boy who rode him, Eddie Arcaro. The jockey set a record in 1952 when he won his fifth Kentucky Derby aboard Hill Gail of the Calumet Farm. Eddie rode ten more years and retired, having won more than thirty million dollars in purses.

Even the old-timers who look back on the twenties as the only period when men were men in sports willingly admit that Big George Mikan (above) was superior to the oldtime basketball heroes. The six-foot, ten-inch forward was twice named on All-American teams at De Paul University and later as a pro on the Minneapolis Lakers (1947–56) he led the National Basketball Association in scoring four years and was named on the N.B.A. All-Star first team for six consecutive seasons. The Mighty Mikan was as graceful as a 245-pound giant could be. He was chosen in the Associated Press mid-century poll as the best hooper in history.

Another stellar performer at the half-century mark was Dick Button, who won the world figure-skating titles for five consecutive years as well as two Olympic crowns (1948 and 1952). Button began skating at the age of eleven in Englewood, New Jersey, and showed such skill that his family took him to Lake Placid that summer to take lessons. Under coach Gus Lussi, young Dick developed the incredible profusion of moves that brought him his first world championship at eighteen. A flawless performer, he constantly dazzled judges with figures no other skater has ever done or even thought of. A model youth, Dick spurned tobacco and liquor in all forms.

A schoolboy prodigy was Bob Mathias, who, at seventeen won the national decathlon championship (in 1948) and went to London to take part in the Olympic Games. He was the youngest American ever to wear an Olympic track suit. Against older and more experienced men, the youth from Tulare, California, emerged the winner in the two-day-long gruelling decathlon (five events each day) and thus become the youngest athlete to win an Olympic track and field event. Back home, the versatile Mathias played football at Stanford and won three more national decathlon championships. In 1952 at the Olympic Games in Helsinki, Finland, he won another gold medal. Bob is the only man who has twice won the Olympic decathlon.

This photograph, taken on August 3, 1952, shows the parade of athletes at the closing ceremonies of the Olympic Games at Helsinki, Finland.

It was the largest of all Olympic Games, with 5,867 athletes from sixty-nine nations competing, and the most successful for the United States in men's track and field, which is the foremost sport in every Olympics.

The Americans also did well in men's swimming (six firsts out of eight events), basketball, weight lifting, and boxing. In the ten weight divisions they won five championships. One of the winners was a seventeen-year-old middleweight with a fast pair of hands named Floyd Patterson.

The year 1952 was an important one in Olympic history, for it marked the entrance of Russia as a serious competitor for the first time. (Russia had sent a small number of entrants to the 1908 and 1912 Olympics and they had won a total of four silver and three bronze medals, mostly in wrestling and shooting—none in track and field, swimming or rowing.)

At Helsinki, however, they were present in full force and it was there that the world's two greatest powers, Russia and the United States, first met head on in track and field (and several other sports) to establish a rivalry that was to grow in intensity and in friendliness.

CHAPTER SIX
The Record Breakers

Throughout the 1950's and well into the next decade the world of sport continued to be crowded with action and excitement. Not since the Golden Age of Sport in the 1920's had so many records been shattered by so many talented athletes, many of whom were too young to vote. Indeed, this new era might be called the Second Golden Age, or perhaps the Era of Record Breakers.

In any event, it was an era that saw soaring attendance figures everywhere, an enormous increase in sports participation, fabulous purses in the professional field, and in the amateur realm a staggering number of individual performances that would have been considered impossible ten years before.

For the first time in American history, gate receipts in sports exceeded one billion dollars annually. The boom reflected in the daily newspapers, which devoted more space to sports than the total coverage given to TV, movies, theater, books, and art. This emphasis on sports caused a few heads to wag in disapproval (as they did in Greece 2,500 years ago when Olympic heroes were glorified to excess) but the newspapers could hardly be blamed for the sports fever. They were simply fulfilling a demand. Sports, as editors well knew, commanded the attention of more participants and spectators than any other recreation.

The new era began, perhaps, with the breakthroughs of the so-called "impenetrable barriers," particularly in track and field and in swimming. The great wave of record-breaking began on May 6, 1954, when England's Roger Bannister smashed the four-minute-mile barrier by running the distance in 3 minutes, 59.4 seconds.

He broke a mile record that had been standing for nine years (Gunder Haegg's 4:01.4 mile set in 1945) but he had scarcely time to catch his breath before his own record was broken—to 3:58 by John Landy of Australia, on June 21, 1954. Bannister opened the floodgates and a deluge came through.

Less than a year later a swarm of milers had broken four minutes fifty times. On the tenth anniversary of Bannister's feat, forty-four men from fifteen nations had run a total of 143 under-four-minute miles.

Meanwhile other world records long considered to be the ultimate in achievement were wiped off the books. These breakthroughs include the twenty-seven-foot broad jump, the seven-foot high jump, the seventeen-foot pole vault, and many others.

Equally impressive were the swimmers who splashed to new records with amazing frequency. Most of these record-breakers were teen-age boys and girls, winners of Olympic gold medals. They were products of the new and successful age-group swimming program for the development of youngsters between the ages of eight and seventeen.

"These kids are going faster from week to week," said Bob Kiphuth. "They simply refuse to be inhibited by long-standing records on the book. Remember Johnny Weismuller's world record of 51 seconds for 100 yards? It was good enough to stay on the books for seventeen years. Why, Johnny couldn't even qualify these days for the National Collegiate Championships. That's how fast swimmers are now."

One of the main reasons for these phenomenal performances in track and swimming is the new concept of training and conditioning. "The whole level of human performance has increased," said Kiphuth. "We now know that the human body can deliver more than anyone ever dreamed of."

The shattering of time-honored records was not confined to amateur sports, of course. Records fell like apples from a tree in major-league baseball and football, hockey, golf, and basketball. On the following pages many of these record breakers are presented.

Here, Roger Bannister breaks the tape at Oxford, England, to become the first man ever to run a mile in less than four minutes. His unprecedented per-formance started a surge of record breaking through-out sports.

America's Bob Hayes, a world record-smasher in the sprints (100 yards, 9.1 sec.; 100 meters, 10 sec. flat), hurls the baton skyward as he wins the 400-meter relay for a world record (39 sec. flat) at the 1964 Olympics.

The prize-winning photo on the opposite page shows pole vaulter John Pennel at the instant he cleared the bar at 17′ ¾″ to to become the first man to vault over 17 feet. His world record, made in August, 1963, was soon bettered.

The star performer of the 1964 Olympics, according to an international poll of sportswriters covering the Games at Tokyo, was eighteen-year-old Don Schollander, who is shown (left) wearing the four gold medals he won for the United States. Not since Jesse Owens (page 207) had an American athlete won four Olympic gold medals, and no swimmer from any country had ever won that many in one set of Games.

The blond youth from Lake Oswego, Oregon, who was on his way to Yale, captured the 100-meter and 400-meter free-style and then swam anchor on the winning 400-meter and 800-meter free-style relay.

Above, Don bangs the finish wall to win the 400-meter relay in the world record time of 3 minutes, 33.2 seconds. He helped set another world mark (7:52.1) in the 800-meter relay, and established still another one in the 400-meter, which he won in 4:12.2. (Johnny Weismuller's best Olympic time for the 400-meter was 52 seconds slower than Don's.)

America's wonderful Water Babies were developed by the nation-wide age-group program and almost all of them were teen-agers. The girls dazzled the world at Tokyo by winning seven of the ten swimming and diving events and shattering four world records while they did.

One of the world marks was set by the four girls shown below, who won the 400-meter medley relay in 4:33.9. From left to right (as they autograph a training float in the Japanese National Gymnasium Pool) they are: Cynthia Goyette of Detroit, Kathlene Ellis of Indianapolis, Cathy Ferguson of Burbank, California, and Sharon Stouder of Glendora, California.

Sharon Stouder, the fifteen-year-old marvel (right, winning the 100-meter butterfly), also swam on two winning relay teams and finished second in the 100-meter free-style. She came home with three gold medals and one silver and was easily the outstanding mermaid of the 1964 Olympics.

Above, Yankee outfielder Roger Maris hits his 61st homer on the final day of the 1961 season to break Babe Ruth's record, made thirty-four years before (page 181). The twenty-seven-year-old Maris and his great teammate, Mickey Mantle, staged the most exciting homerun duel in history that season.

Mickey finished with 54 homers and a batting average of .314. Roger batted only .269 but because of his 61 homers he was voted the league's Most Valuable Player as well as the Number One Male Athlete in the Nation by an Associated Press poll.

However, after the shouting had died down, the validity of Maris' record was questioned. The reason: Maris, playing a 162-game season (extended from 154 games because of the expansion of the American League to ten teams in 1961), had an eight-game advantage over Ruth. Maris did not hit his 61 homers in 154 games, as Ruth had done, and therefore did not break Ruth's record. So decreed Baseball Commissioner Ford Frick. Some agreed with Frick; others did not, arguing with some justification that, after all, a "season" is a "season" and there should be no double standard in statistics.

One of the most durable of all baseball records (Ty Cobb's 96 stolen bases in 1915, page 128) bit the dust in 1962 when the Los Angeles Dodgers' wiry shortstop, Maury Wills (below, sliding), stole 104 bases. But was it really a record? Again Commissioner Frick came forth with some cloudy reasoning. Wills didn't do it in 154 games, said Frick, and put a footnote on the record.

But many other baseball records were broken that no one could question as the Yankees, as usual, kept rolling along at the top. They won ten flags in the twelve-year period that Casey Stengel managed them (1949–60), three more for manager Ralph Houk (1961–63) and in 1964 one for Yogi Berra, who was promptly fired. More than ever, the American League had become a one-team league.

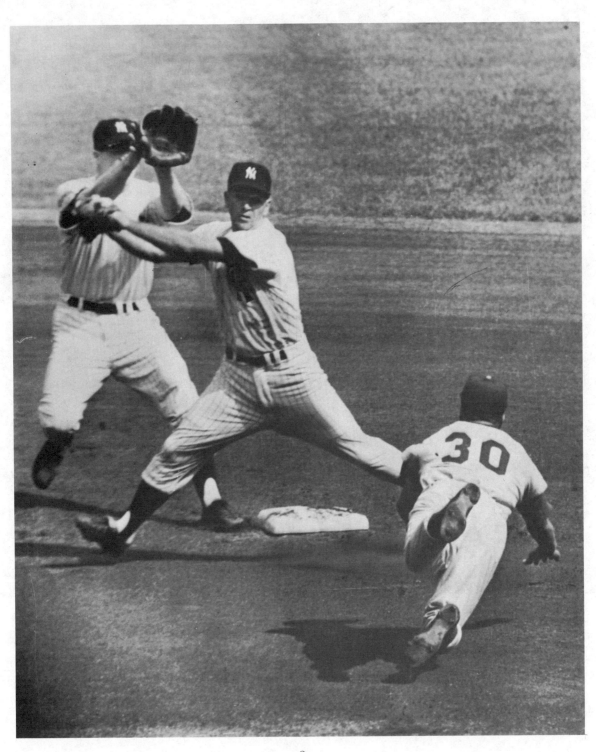

Casey Stengel, shown here with a photo of Yogi Berra, the former Yankee catcher and manager, was an extremely popular figure during his twelve years with the Bombers. In that time he brought seven World Championships to New York. No Yankee manager before him had ever been that successful. Nevertheless, Casey was cold-bloodedly dropped by the Yankee brass shortly after the World Series of 1960. Sportswriters and fans were stunned. Casey himself was crushed.

But Casey was not through. He was made manager of the New York Mets, the National League team that replaced the Giants after they fled to San Francisco. Playing in Shea Stadium (below), a splendid ball park with all modern conveniences, the Mets immediately caught on in New York. Even though they were probably the worst ball club in the majors, they became more popular than the pennant-winning Yankees and outdrew them by a whopping margin in their own home town.

Despite the many fine Yankee players, most fans saw the club as a stuffy business organization. The image was not improved when the Columbia Broadcasting System bought the Bombers. This was part of the changing scene in the structure of baseball. It included the many franchise switches, the abandonment of New York by the Giants and Dodgers, the hopping of the Braves from Boston to Milwaukee to Atlanta, and the botched-up records due to the long season.

George S. Halas (left), coach and owner of the Chicago Bears, was largely responsible for the phenomenal rise in popularity of professional football. Should it ever replace baseball as the national pastime (and there are strong indications it may), the game can thank Halas.

His signing of Red Grange in 1925 started the game's rise (page 163) and Halas kept it going. His inventive mind revived and redesigned the old T formation, thus giving the game an explosive attack and leading the way into a new era. With it, Halas' Bears beat the Washington Redskins 73–0 in the 1940 championship playoff game. In 1963, when Halas was sixty-eight, he won his eighth championship by defeating the Giants 14–10.

"Pro football," the experts often say, "is a game of infinite complexity." This is illustrated in the photo above which shows Giant quarterback, Y. A. Tittle, directing a last-minute shift in strategy just before the ball is snapped.

Off his feet but still going strong, blockbuster Jim Brown zooms through the line to add another rushing record to the numerous ones already in his book. This photo points out why the Cleveland Browns' magnificent fullback has been rated by experts as the greatest ball carrier football has ever known.

The six-foot, two-inch super athlete was All-American at Syracuse University in the mid-1950's and also starred in basketball, lacrosse and track.

Coach Blanton Collier of the Browns once said of Jim: "He's not only the greatest football player I've ever seen; he's the greatest athlete."

Safety man Don Burroughs of the Philadelphia Eagles had a different view of the 228-pound Cleveland bulldozer. "Every time I tackle Jimmy Brown," he said, "I hear a dice game going on inside my mouth."

Jim came to Cleveland in 1957 and for five straight seasons led the National Football League in yards gained rushing. He slipped to fourth place in 1962 (due to a sprained left wrist) but he was back on top again the next two years. In 1964 he entered a brand new record bracket: the 10,000-yard club. No back ever gained that much. Jim is the only member of the club. His awesome blend of speed and crushing power kept Cleveland at the top.

This photo of Pasadena's Rose Bowl jammed with 98,214 spectators on New Year's Day, 1962 (Minnesota 23, UCLA 3), illustrates the popularity of the college game.

The Rose Bowl game, incidentally, is the second most popular televised sporting event every year in the United States, the first being the World Series.

College football attendance shot through the 20,000,000 mark for the first time in 1960 and continued to climb. In 1963, despite cancellation of several games because of President Kennedy's death, attendance rose to 22,237,094.

As for the pro game, the two rival leagues (National and American) enjoyed an unbelievable television bonanza in 1965 when competing networks showered them with gold.

In January, the Columbia Broadcasting System paid $28.2 million for a two-year contract for the rights to the 98 regular-season games of the N.F.L. Two weeks later the National Broadcasting Company shelled out $36 million for the A.F.L. schedule of 56 games over a five-year period beginning in 1965. Rich beyond their dreams, the leagues began bidding for collegiate talent.

The sports world was stunned at the price the New York Jets, an American League club, paid for Alabama's quarterback, Joe Namath (shown here with his college coach, Paul Bryant). It was $405,000, the highest price ever paid for a rookie in the history of pro football, perhaps the highest ever paid for an untested athlete in any sport, anywhere. Joe more than earned his salary when he led the Jets to victory over the Baltimore Colts in the 1969 Super Bowl game in Miami.

Rocky Marciano won the heavyweight title from Jersey Joe Walcott in 1952, defended it six times and retired undefeated in 1956. An elimination tournament for the vacant crown held that year was won by twenty-one-year-old Floyd Patterson, the youngest man ever to win the championship. He also became the youngest to lose it, which he did on June 25, 1959, when he was K.O.'d by Ingemar Johansson of Sweden. But Floyd regained his crown a year later by stopping the Swede (above) in the fifth round.

Floyd must be listed with the record breakers, for despite his unimpressive ring career (he met a string of second-raters while champion), he did regain his lost championship, which is something no other heavyweight had ever done.

For some time he had avoided meeting Sonny Liston (right), the number one challenger, because of the latter's unsavory past. Sonny had served time for armed robbery and was a head-knocking labor goon hired by gangsters.

There was not much to the bout, which was held in Chicago in September, 1962. Floyd went down and out in the first round and Sonny was champion.

They met again less than a year later (July 22, 1963, at Las Vegas, Nevada) and again the battle was a farce.

The above photo shows what happened. Floyd did not last the first round.

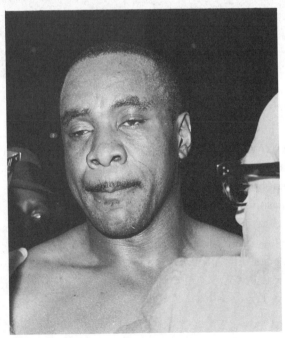

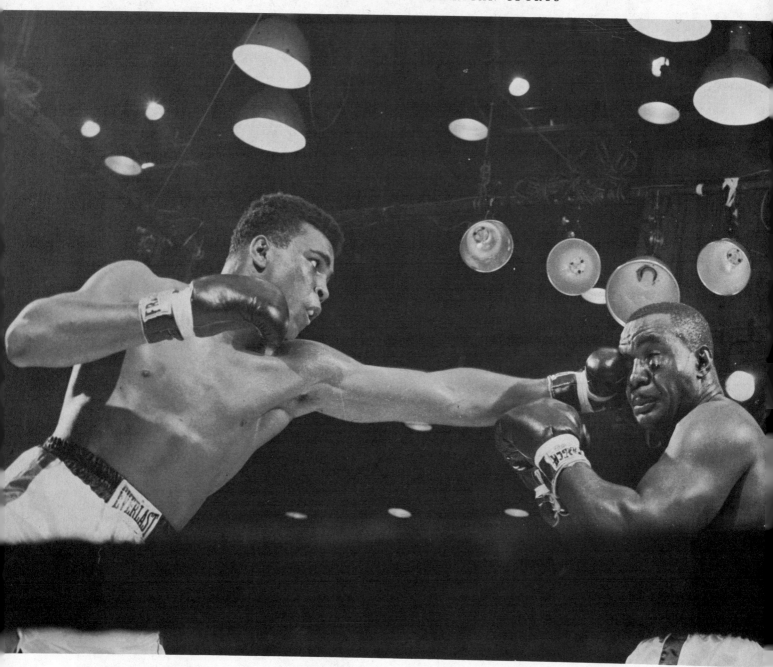

The boxing writers went into a trance after Liston destroyed Patterson the second time. They rated the champion along with the ring's greatest heavyweights, pictured him as invincible, capable of smashing a dinosaur with one swipe of his mighty fist.

There was nobody fighting who had any chance against him, they wrote, although that youngster from Louisville with the unusual name of Cassius Marcellus Clay might last a little longer than Floyd had. And who was Cassius?

He was a blabber-mouth, only twenty-two years old, but he had a good amateur record (Olympic light heavyweight champion, 1960) and he had a pair of lightning-fast hands, a beautiful build, and he was supremely confident. He stood six feet, three inches, and weighed 210 pounds.

The odds on Liston soared to nearly 10 to 1 when the two met at Miami Beach on February 25, 1964. It was even money that Liston would win by a K.O. in six rounds. What Cassius did to Sonny is shown in the above photo.

Dancing out of reach and stabbing Sonny with a punishing left jab, Cassius made the scowling and bewildered champion look foolish. Sonny kept plodding after his man, swinging wildly, but he could not find him. "Come on, you big bum, come on!" taunted the light-footed Cassius as he kept circling to his left. Liston vainly pawed the air.

Clay wanted to quit at the beginning of the fifth round when he was blinded by rubbing fluid, but his trainer made him go on. His eyes cleared up and he gave Liston a heavy pounding. At the end of the sixth round a weary Liston sat on his stool and quit cold. In their next fight, in 1965, Clay won by a K.O. in the first round with a short right.

Arnold Palmer, the world's best known and most popular golfer of the early 1960's, is in the front center, in the above photo, pursued by his ever-present and often unruly gallery known as "Arnie's Army." A closer view of the colorful professional (left) shows him agonizing over a missed putt.

Many were the reasons for his tremendous crowd appeal: his fresh good looks, his poise and good humor, his bold attack, and, of course, his superb game. Playing go-for-broke golf, Palmer won the U.S. Open (1960), the British Open twice (1961–62) and the Masters a record-breaking four times (1958–60–62–64).

In an era of fantastic purses, Palmer became a millionaire almost overnight. In 1963 he was golf's leading money winner, earning $128,230 in P.G.A.-sanctioned tournaments, yet he did not win a major tournament that year. His total earnings, including endorsements, exhibitions, and movies totaled about $750,000 in 1963.

"Champagne" Tony Lema (right), a slim Californian who earned his nickname because of his habit of toasting his victories with champagne, was one of a group of outstanding young players who brightened the fairways in the 1960's. A former cannery worker, Tony came up through the ranks to become one of the five or six best golfers in the world. He won the British Open (and purses totaling $74,130.-37) in 1964.

Big Jack Nicklaus (below), Arnold Palmer's chief rival and good friend, won the U.S. Amateur twice (1959 and 1961) and in his first year as a pro (1962) won the U.S. Open. He was then only twenty-two and had two terms left at Ohio State. A powerhouse and terrific driver, Jack went on from there, locking horns with Palmer in numerous tournaments and alternately beating him and losing to him.

The pendulum swung in Jack's favor in 1964 when he became top money winner with $113,285.50, or $81.13 more than Palmer won.

Among the record breakers of the era was the great thoroughbred, Kelso (on the left, hitting the finish line with Gun Bow), who established a world record for lifetime earnings in 1964 by winning a total of $1,893,362. Kelso was voted Horse-of-the-Year for the fifth consecutive year in 1964, another record.

Kelso's counterpart among the standardbreds was Adios Butler, holder of more records than any other sulky-pulling horse.

At the end of his competitive career, The Butler had thirty-seven victories in fifty starts, earnings of more than a half a million dollars, and had set world pacing records for the mile, mile and a sixteenth, and mile and an eighth.

The Butler helped make harness horse racing the big sport it is. Crowds of more than 50,000 gather for the big events, and the sport annually attracts more spectators than major-league baseball. In 1963 more than 24,000,000 people saw the sulky-pullers, while less than 21,000,000 fans attended big-league baseball games.

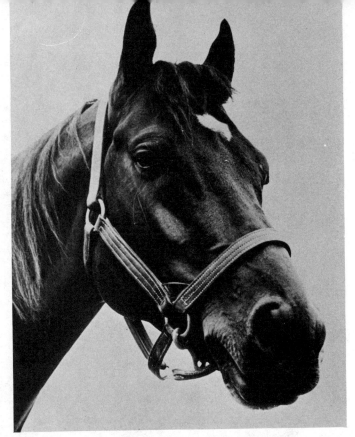

Opposite: Wilton (Wilt the Stilt) Chamberlain, professional basketball's greatest scorer and the only man ever to drop in a hundred points in one game, makes one of his typical dunk shots in a National Basketball Association game. The seven-foot, one-inch, center was paid up to $70,000 a year, the highest salary in the game's history.

The Boston Celtics, however, without Wilt to help them but with the equally great Bob Cousy, ran up a winning record unmatched in professional sports in 1964 when they won the world championship for the sixth year in a row, thus topping the New York Yankees five straight (1949–53) World Series victories.

When Chuck McKinley (right) and Dennis Ralston (left) brought the Davis Cup back to the United States from Australia in December, 1963, they were greeted with jubilation and excitement. The two college youths had combined to eke out a 3-2 victory, thus ending Australia's five-year domination.

Unlike almost all other sports in the United States, tennis suffered a decline in the 1950's. There was a dearth of talent and attendance fell off everywhere. Tennis fans had high hopes that McKinley and Ralston, both in their early twenties, would keep the cup for years, but it went back to Australia in 1964.

The year 1964 may have been bad for American tennis but it was a good one for yacht racing. It was the year that the United States 12-meter yacht *Constellation* defeated Britain's *Sovereign* and maintained possession of the America's Cup, symbol of world leadership in yacht racing.

The big sloop was skippered by Eric Ridder (right) of Locust Valley, New York. The helmsman, Robert N. Bavier, Jr., of Darien, Connecticut, is in the photo below wearing a white cap. This picture was taken during the second race of the match in rough seas off Newport, Rhode Island.

The series turned out to be a dismal mismatch. The British challenger was defeated in four straight races and was never close in any of them.

Althea Gibson, who started out playing paddle tennis on the streets of Harlem, was the first Negro to be invited to the U.S. Lawn Tennis Association's National Championship. She made her Forest Hills debut in 1950 but was eliminated in the second round.

After seven years of trying, she finally made it—at the age of thirty. Tall and lean, she became the world's best woman tennis player. In 1957–58, her peak years, she won two U.S. National Championships and was twice winner at Wimbledon, tennis' brightest crown.

The Era of Record Breakers produced many top-notch women athletes, some of whom are shown on the following pages. Mary Katherine (Mickey) Wright (above), holder of innumerable golf records, earned universal recognition as the best woman golfer of all time.

Winner of her fourth U.S. Women's Open in 1964, all-time leading money winner ($176,994, career total in 1964) and recipient of the Female Athlete of the Year award in 1963, Mickey once shot a 62 in tournament play. It was the finest round of golf ever played by a woman.

Above, Wilma Rudolph gets off to a flying start in the 200-meter dash at the 1960 Olympic Games in Rome. The fleet-footed American girl, who set world records in the sprints at various distances during her brief career, won three gold medals at Rome—the most ever won by an American woman in track and field in any Olympics. Wilma won the 100 meters, the 200 meters, and anchored the women's 400-meter relay team, which won in the world-record time of 44.4 seconds.

Right, Donna Mae Mims adjusts her pink crash helmet as she sits in her bright pink Austin-Healey Sprite before the start of a race. An accomplished race driver, the striking platinum blonde is the first woman to win a Sports Car Club of America championship. This she did in 1964 in competition with thirty-one men in the Class H production category for imported two-seaters. On the back of Donna Mae's car her motto was written in bold lettering: THINK PINK.

Leonore Modell (above) astonished and delighted the world on September 3, 1964, when she swam the English Channel (in 15 hours, 32 seconds). There was nothing remarkable about her time, but there was about her age.

She was only fourteen years old. Leonore, a 135-pound high school student of Sacramento, California, is the youngest person ever to conquer the Channel. Officials of the Channel Association called the swim "epic."

CHAPTER SEVEN
The Era of the Pros

When the Houston Astrodome opened its doors in 1965, weather ceased to be a factor for the first time in the long history of baseball. Rain, fog, wet grounds, and heat no longer existed for the fans and players within the domed, covered stadium.

It was the most important innovation since the first major-league night game was played in Cincinnati in 1935. The luxurious 44,500-seat home of the Astros of the National League took four years to build and cost 32 million dollars. The electric scoreboard alone cost 2 million dollars—almost as much as the Yankee Stadium cost when it was built in 1923.

The Astrodome was perhaps symbolic of the rise and continued momentum of professional sport in the late 1960s and early '70s.

It was a time of super stadiums, super salaries, and superstars. It was also a time of franchise jumping, uncontrolled expansion, and league warfare among the Big Four of team sports—baseball, football, basketball, and hockey.

The superstars became walking corporations, followed by their bag carriers, lawyers, publishers, and business agents.

The Yankee dynasty ended in the sixties. For 43 years the Bronx Bombers had dominated the American League. They had won 29 pennants and 20 world championships, but their collapse was in sight. After winning their fifth straight flag in 1964, they skidded to sixth place the next year, then tumbled to the bottom a year later, 26½ games off the pace.

With their downfall came the upsurge of the National League, which had long played second fiddle to the American. The Nationals won six of the 10 World Series and 11 of the 12 all-star games played during the sixties. In the 10-year stretch from 1964 to 1973 they won nine out of 10 all-star games.

The National League excelled in every department of the game. It produced more base stealers, more .300 hitters and more home-run sluggers than the rival league, and its pitching was superior.

Its strength came in great part from the many blacks within its fold. Ever since Jackie Robinson —the first Negro to play major-league ball in this century—joined the Dodgers in 1947, the National League has attracted an increasing number of blacks.

Baseball celebrated its 100th anniversary in 1969, dating its birth to the Cincinnati Red Stockings of 1869, the first professional team.

The year 1969 saw a big change in the game's structure as both leagues expanded to 12 clubs and each league was split into two six-team divisions (Eastern and Western).

In an effort to increase attendance by producing more hits and runs, the American League adopted a new rule in 1973 called the "designated hitter." It allowed a player (almost always the pitcher) to remain in the game while a substitute batted in his place. The substitute was the designated hitter, supposedly a slugger. He did nothing but bat. The new rule was to be in effect for three years on an experimental basis and if successful might be adopted by the National League, which was consistently outdrawing the American at the gate.

Professional football continued to grow in strength, and the 1972-73 season saw the greatest record ever recorded by a pro team in this sport. The Miami Dolphins went 17 and 0, winning 14 regular season games, two NFC playoff games, and the Super Bowl. Other teams had won all of their regular season games but Miami was the first team to continue unbeaten through the playoffs.

By 1973 there were a total of 105 clubs engaged in professional major sports, a staggering number by any count. A sports editor recently listed the nicknames of the 105 teams and defied his readers to identify half of them without consulting the record books.

Playing for these teams were roughly 2,500 trained athletes, many of whom commanded salaries that corporation presidents would envy. Some, who had yet to see 35, were millionaires.

Altogether about 25 baseball players were earning at least $100,000 a year and this does not include the side benefits they received from endorsements and speaking appearances. Basketball players came even higher on the market, as did the superstars of hockey and football.

For example, in July of 1973 Gordie Howe, the symbol of hockey in Detroit for 28 years, changed leagues and signed a four-year contract for one million dollars to play with his two sons for the Houston Aeros of the World Hockey Association. Howe left behind him 13 records in the National Hockey League book. He was the league's all-time leading scorer with 876 goals.

Not long afterward, Julius Erving, a star basketball forward, was obtained from the Virginia Squires by the New York Nets for a record 3.5 million dollars. Erving signed an eight-year contract for an undisclosed amount, but it probably was in excess of a previous contract that called for $200,000 the first year and escalated to $260,-000 the fifth year.

The unprecedented boom in sports plus inflation brought about these fantastic salaries. High as they are, these amounts are mere peanuts compared to the purse split between two gladiators when they met in the prize ring on the night of March 8, 1971.

The build-up for the purse began back in the mid-sixties when heavyweight champion Cassius Clay (soon to become Muhammad Ali) successfully defended his crown by defeating in order Floyd Patterson, George Chuvalo, Henry Cooper, Brian London, Karl Mildenberger, Cleveland Williams, Ernie Terrell, and Zora Folley.

His fight with Folley on March 22, 1967, was Clay's 29th consecutive victory without a defeat or draw, and his ninth defense of his title. He had shown that he was truly a "fighting champion" of magnificent boxing skill. But his career was abruptly halted in June, 1967, when he was sentenced to five years in prison for refusing to serve in the United States armed forces.

Within hours various state and foreign boxing commissions stripped him of his title. The deposed champion announced his retirement and declared that his title was now "vacated."

In the next three years the heavyweight crown was sought and claimed by several fighters but nothing was settled until February 16, 1970, when the two best active claimants met in a bout for the championship.

They were Jimmy Ellis and Joe Frazier. Joe was the 4 to 1 favorite and he lived up to those odds by stopping Ellis in a one-sided battle.

Frazier was immediately recognized as the undisputed world champion by all boxing organizations in this country and abroad. It was not difficult to accept Frazier, for he was a formidable fighting machine, an aggressive, forward-moving puncher whose attack never ceased. And he had an unblemished record. The former Olympic champion had never known defeat since he turned pro in 1965.

Clay decided to return to the ring in 1970 and announced that he was the "real" heavyweight champion. The Supreme Court had overturned his draft conviction and the way was clear. It was now obvious that Clay-Ali and Joe Frazier were on a collision course. Both had disposed of all pretenders to the throne. They alone stood on the summit.

This was a unique situation in boxing history—two undefeated fighters with claims to the championship and each at the peak of his career.

The two champions signed to fight in Madison Square Garden in New York on March 8, 1970 for the largest purse in the annals of boxing. Each fighter was guaranteed 2.5 million dollars, win, lose, or draw. No athlete in any sport had ever received that much money for a single performance.

The battle would be shown in the United States and Canada in 337 theaters on television and would be beamed by satellite to 46 nations. It would be seen by about 300 million viewers around the world. Total gate receipts would be 23 million dollars—sport's biggest payday, ever.

The fight was a thriller, a classic pairing of boxer and slugger—Ali, the boxing master and stylist, against the crouching aggressor punching with both hands.

Ali pierced Joe's defense with neat left jabs but Joe kept boring in, his head bobbing, throwing hooks to the head and body. This was the pattern of the entire fight, which lasted 15 rounds.

In the final round Joe caught Ali with a powerful left hook to the jaw and put him on his back, but Ali quickly got to his feet and was standing at the finish. Joe was declared the winner by the unanimous decision of the two judges and the referee. It was clearly Joe's fight and he was now the undisputed heavyweight champion of the world.

Joe and Ali went their separate ways after the "Battle of the Century." Joe fought only twice in 1972, both times against unknown and unranked pugs, neither of whom lasted four rounds. His perfect record was now: 29 fights, 29 won (25 won by K.O.).

It would seem that the powerful champion would wear his crown for years, but this was not to be so.

On January 22, 1973, in Kingston, Jamaica, Joe's crown was knocked off his head by big George Foreman in one of the most stunning upsets in ring history. Foreman, the 1968 Olympic champion and unbeaten pro, knocked Joe down six times in the first two rounds before the referee stopped the slaughter in the second.

The new Texas-born champion maintained his perfect record by stopping Joe: 38 straight victories, 35 of which he won by knockouts.

Golf and tennis offered tremendous rewards in tournament money and gave rise to a new group of affluent young men and women. Some of the top golfers flew their own planes as they pursued the richest golf tournaments on the Professional Golf Association circuit.

Jack Nicklaus became the first golfer to win more than a quarter of a million dollars in one year, when he pocketed $244,490.50 in 1971. (Ten years before, Gary Player was the leading money winner with $64,540.45.)

Currently the Big Four of international golf are Jack Nicklaus, Arnold Palmer, Gary Player, and Lee Trevino. Palmer is still the favorite of the crowds, along with Lee Trevino, the Merry Mexican.

A former caddy and golf hustler, the Mexican-American drops wisecracks and kids with the gallery between shots. Trevino has twice won the U.S. Open, also the British Open twice.

Big-time tennis has turned completely pro and the world's top players are now paid above the table instead of underneath it for appearing at Wimbledon, Forest Hills, and other posh establishments. This means that even the Davis Cup players play for pay, which is a horrible thought to some purists, but not to the average tennis buff and the sports world in general.

In any event, some topnotch tennis has developed in this country and the long dominance of the game by Australia seems to be dissolving.

The United States has won the Davis Cup five years in a row since 1968. Stan Smith and Billie Jean King, the American aces, can hold their own against the world's best. Billie Jean won her fifth Wimbledon singles title in 1973 and added the women's doubles and the mixed doubles championships for a clean sweep and three trophies. She has won three U.S. singles titles and innumerable other championships in world tennis.

Smith's many titles include U.S. and British (Wimbledon) championships and the World Championship of Tennis on the pro tour.

The annual earnings of the top-ranking male pros such as Smith, Arthur Ashe, the American black, and the Australians, Ken Rosenwall, Rod Laver, and John Newcombe, hover around $100,-000. The figure does not include side benefits, which are considerable.

Every generation or so a racehorse thunders down the stretch and excites the nation. In 1919 it was Man O' War; in 1948 it was Citation, the first million-dollar horse. Now it is Secretariat, who might be called a six-million-dollar horse because that is what a syndicate paid owner Mrs. John (Penny) Tweedy for the magnificent Thoroughbred (actually $6,080,000). Like Man O' War, he is a strapping, chestnut colt and is also nicknamed "Big Red."

He was a sensation from the start, winning seven of nine races as a two-year-old, in 1972. He opened the 1973 season with two convincing victories, then lost the Wood Memorial Stakes. Thereafter he joined the immortals of the racetrack by winning the Triple Crown in the most brilliant performance ever known on the American turf:

The fastest Kentucky Derby in history, 1:59 2/5 for the 1 1/4 miles; a Preakness triumph that carried him from last place going into the first turn into the lead coming out of it and winning in the second-best time for that traditional race; an incredible time of 2:24 for the Belmont, thereby smashing the record by 2 3/5 seconds (the equivalent of 13 lengths) and winning by 31 lengths. He was so far ahead at the finish that the TV cameras could not show the rest of the field. Secretariat thus became the first Triple Crown winner since Citation turned the trick in 1948.

Ever since the Russians entered the Olympics in earnest in 1952 the games have become largely a two-nation rivalry—America vs. Russia. The United States, understandably, had the advantage over the newcomers and surpassed them in almost every field. But as time went on the gap began to close, especially in track and field, the showcase Olympic sport, in which the United States had been supreme since the modern games began.

No longer is this so. In both the winter and summer games the Russians have forged ahead and America's dominance in track and field has ended.

This was most evident in the Munich Games in 1972, a record low for American male athletes who won only six gold medals in the 24 track and field events. The American women fared even worse. For the first time ever they failed to win a single gold medal.

The one bright spot for America in an Olympics marred by disaster and tragedy as 11 Israeli athletes were murdered by Arab fanatics, was in swimming.

In the 29 swimming events, America's excep-tional men and women captured a total of 17 gold medals, eight of which were won by women.

The brightest star was Mark Spitz, who won seven golds and all of them in world record time —four in individual events, three in relays. No other swimmer, or athlete in any sport for that matter, had ever reached such Olympian heights.

The world's greatest swimmer was not everybody's hero, however. He had never been very popular among his fellow Olympians. At a news conference in Munich right after his final victory he offended reporters by being "snide and flippant," according to *Newsweek* magazine, and "refusing to pose for the one picture everybody wanted to see—showing all seven medals around his neck. . . . It turned out that Spitz was trying to sell that prized picture to a magazine." Spitz became an instant millionaire shortly after the Olympics by signing a contract with a Hollywood talent agency.

Index